ENCOURAGING CITIZENSHIP

Report of the
Commission on Citizenship

LONDON: HMSO

ISBN 0 11 701485 0

Contents

SECTION I

What Citizenship Means: The Commission's Starting Point

SECTION II

Impediments to Citizenship

SECTION III

Encouraging Citizenship

Foreword

by the Right Hon. Bernard Weatherill M.P.
Speaker of the House of Commons
Patron of the Commission on Citizenship

If you have time for a brief visit to the British Museum you will find on display in the Manuscript Saloon on the ground floor an original copy of the Magna Carta agreed by King John on 15 June 1215. It is an inspiring document to read, concluding as it does that 'the English Church shall be free, and that men in our kingdom shall have and keep all these liberties, rights and concessions well and peaceably in their fullness and entirety . . . in all things and in all places for ever . . . given by our hand in the meadow that is called Runnymede'.

Magna Carta represented a step – an important one – in the long process of establishing a free society for men and women here in Britain. The great international human rights charters and conventions to which our country is a signatory and which are reproduced in this Report are further steps in that process which is still going on. Great changes are affecting our society today, but at a faster pace than ever before. All of us, but in particular our young people, need to be alert to the implications of these changes for our freedoms.

I have always made a special point of showing young people around the House of Commons and meeting and talking with them, both to introduce them to the way in which our country is governed, and to find out their feelings and opinions on this subject. However, I have often found that many of our intelligent and serious young people have little idea of how they are governed, nor what part they themselves might play in that process. The future of our society is in the hands of these young people and others like them.

I believe that citizenship, like anything else, has to be learned. Young people do not become good citizens by accident, any more than they become good nurses, or good engineers, or good bus drivers, or computer scientists. My concern about whether we offer enough encouragement to our young people to learn how to be good citizens was a major reason why I was glad to be Patron of the Commission on Citizenship. With that in mind, I congratulate the Commission on the two major achievements it already has to its credit.

The first concerns the teaching of citizenship in schools. From the start the Commission publicly advocated that a place should be found for citizenship studies in the curriculum. The Commission's education team based at Leicester University has done pioneering work. A survey by the Commission discovered that teaching about citizenship in schools was very uneven. The national consultative conference that followed the survey established the basics for the Commission's evidence to the National Curriculum Council. The National Curriculum Council, supported by both Government and Opposition, has now declared citizenship to be one of the five cross-curricular themes that schools should take into account, and that it plans to issue guidelines on the subject. This is good news. Teachers can and should tell students about the freedoms we enjoy and how we came by them. They can encourage young people to acquire and practice the basic skills of citizenship. I mean the ability to argue a case fairly and calmly, to represent others or to work in a team, to negotiate and plan together.

Secondly, young people at the outset of their adult lives need to be offered the *experience* of working with others to tackle and solve real problems in their own local environment. I believe that that kind of experience of involvement, of belonging, of sharing responsibility, is a crucial element in the process of learning to be a good citizen. I am pleased that the Commission on Citizenship, working with the Prince's Trust, has been able to contribute to the development of the new scheme 'Volunteers', which was launched by the Prince of Wales and myself on 25th April at St James' Palace. 'Volunteers' aims to give every young person who so wishes the opportunity to complete a period of voluntary service in the community.

This Report is not confined to citizenship among young people. The Commission on Citizenship, an all-Party body whose members are drawn from all walks of public life, has considered what is meant by citizenship and how this applies to the public institutions of our society and to the great range of voluntary bodies and independent associations, and above all, to individual citizens of all ages. I warmly congratulate and thank the Commission and all who worked with them and helped them in the preparation of this thought provoking report which I think will contribute to a wide public debate on these important matters.

Membership of the Commission

Peter Jenkins	Headmaster, Ashburton High School, Croydon; Principal Designate, Bacon's CTC, London Docklands
Alison Kelly	Secretary, National Association of Governors and Managers
John Lyles	Chairman of S Lyles plc for the CBI
John Monks	Deputy General Secretary, TUC
Rt. Rev. Peter Mumford	Bishop of Truro (now retired)
Jonathan Porritt	Director, Friends of the Earth
John Rea Price	Director of Islington Social Services, President of the Association of Directors of Social Services
Richard Pulford	Former CSV Volunteer, now student at Sidney Sussex College, Cambridge
Andrew Rowe	Member of Parliament, Mid Kent (Conservative)
Kim Taylor	Former Headmaster of Sevenoaks School and former Director of the Calouste Gulbenkian Foundation (UK Branch)
Martin Tims	Esso UK plc
Rt. Rev. Howard Tripp	Auxiliary Bishop of Southwark
Ben Whitaker	Director of The Calouste Gulbenkian Foundation (UK Branch) and former Member of Parliament
Professor Ted Wragg	Director of School of Education, Exeter University
Frances Morrell	Secretary to the Commission

Observer:

Richard Fries	Home Office

Introduction

The Commission was set up in December 1988. Its Members and Secretary were appointed by the Speaker of the House of Commons.

The Aims and Objects of the Commission

The aim of the Commission was to consider how best to encourage, develop and recognise Active Citizenship within a wide range of groups in the community, both local and national, including school students, adults, those in full employment as well as volunteers.
     The Commission initially set itself the following tasks:

- to define citizenship, including active citizenship

- to review existing initiatives in this area

- to examine the advantages and disadvantages of different kinds of recognition, and to develop criteria for recognition

- to review possible forms of recognition for individuals, groups and organisations, such as accreditation, awards and assessments.

Method of Working

During the period from January 1989 to July 1990 the Commission held seven one-day meetings, and two weekend seminars. A Commission Working Party met regularly to co-ordinate the Commission's programme.

The Commission's Approach

From the beginning the Commission decided to work with others and to draw upon experience and knowledge gained during this joint work. The organisations which worked in partnership with the Commission included the British Institute for International and Comparative Law, the Centre for the Study of Comprehensive Schools, the Family Policy Studies Unit, the Industry and Parliament Trust, Leicester University, the Policy Studies Institute,

Members of the Faculty of Political and Social Sciences at Cambridge University, the Prince's Trust and Social and Community Planning Research (SCPR).

The Commission drew on a number of seminars, conferences and meetings, and specially prepared papers.

Philosophy of Citizenship

Commission Members attended a private seminar on the Philosophy of Citizenship at St Antony's College, Oxford. The Speaker of the House of Commons, Bernard Weatherill MP and the then Home Secretary, Douglas Hurd MP spoke at the Seminar. Papers were given by Sir Ralf Dahrendorf, Warden of St Antony's, Paul Boateng MP, Professor Barry of Buckingham University, Roger Henderson QC, and Professor Plant of Southampton University.

Constitutional and legal implications of citizenship

Piers Gardner, Director of the British Institute of International and Comparative Law, advised the Commission on legal and constitutional matters, and prepared the Commission paper published as part of this Report. The paper was considered at a joint seminar held at the Institute.

Independent associations and volunteers in society

A review of evidence on 'Active Citizenship' was prepared by Janet Edwards of Leicester University. A review of evidence on 'Active Citizenship and a Healthy Society' was prepared by David Halpern of St John's College, Cambridge.

Citizenship and caring

Malcolm Wicks, Director of the Family Policy Studies Centre, advised the Commission on this issue, and two discussion meetings were held at the Centre.

Citizenship and schools

A working party was established which met regularly at Leicester University. Its members were: Frances Morrell (*Chair*), Professor Fogelman (Director of Research), Martin Tims, George Gyte, Sue Harrison, Stan Bryce (Centre for the Study of Comprehensive Schools).

A national survey of schools was carried out by Professor Fogelman and Social and Community Planning Research (SCPR). An in-depth study of schools in Leicestershire and

Northamptonshire was carried out under the guidance of Professor Fogelman, George Gyte and Sue Harrison.

A national consultative conference was organised for the Commission by the Centre for the Study of Comprehensive Schools. Evidence was submitted to the National Curriculum Council, for consideration by the Council before the NCC guidance on citizenship in schools was circulated.

Young Volunteers in the Community

A working party was established composed of Sir John Cassels (*Chair*), Tom Shebbeare (Director of the Prince's Trust), Hilary Omissi (Prince's Trust) and Frances Morrell. The Working Party met regularly at the Prince's Trust.

A series of joint consultations, chaired by Sir Richard O'Brien, was held at the Policy Studies Institute. A consultative document 'Young Volunteers in the Community' was published jointly by the Prince's Trust and the Commission. A jointly sponsored scheme, 'Volunteers', was launched by the Prince of Wales at a conference in St James' Palace, chaired by the Speaker.

50+ Volunteering

The Commission held consultations with the 50+ Volunteering Group. They were: Jill Munday (*Chair*) (REACH), Len Ferris (Shell UK), Deirdre Wynne-Harley (Centre for Policy on Ageing), Peter Bryant (Wales Council for Voluntary Action), Janet Atfield (RSVP), Gwynfi Jones (The Emeritus Register), Peter Jewell (Age Link), Liz Robertson (Volunteer Development, Scotland), Joyce Colston (National Association of Volunteer Bureaux), Frances Cook (Age Concern), Mark Rankin (Secretary) (Volunteer Centre UK).

The Youth Service

A paper on the place of citizenship in the core curriculum of the Youth Service was prepared by the National Youth Bureau for the Commission. Frances Morrell contributed to a national conference organised by the NYB on behalf of the Department of Education and Science on the subject of citizenship within the core curriculum.

Higher education

A survey of those selecting students for courses of higher education was undertaken by Dr Mary Hallaway and Malcolm Deere. The purpose of the survey was to ascertain whether voluntary service to the community was a factor in the selection of students for courses.

A seminar organised by Malcolm Deere was held at Senate House, London University. John Francis prepared a paper summarising the results of the survey, by comparison with the survey of employers carried out by the Industry and Parliament Trust. The summary is printed as Appendix F.

Industry

The Commission worked with the Industry and Parliament Trust on the question of Industry and Citizenship. Frederick Hyde Chambers (Director) and Martin Tims prepared and circulated a survey on this question. A Seminar of industrialists was organised by the Trust at the House of Commons, and a paper prepared by Frederick Hyde Chambers on the outcome of the survey and consultations.

Advice and criticism

Members and post-graduate researchers of the Social and Political Sciences Faculty of Cambridge University offered criticism and advice throughout the development of the Report. They were: Ray Jobling (Chair of the Faculty), David Halpern, Katherine Fieldback, Mike Jones, Tom Shakespeare, Yvonne Summers and William Watson.

Stockport Metropolitan Borough Council held a one day consultative seminar.

Acknowledgements

The Commission gratefully acknowledges the support of the following bodies: Community Service Volunteers, Esso UK plc, the Gulbenkian Foundation, Northamptonshire County Council and Leicestershire County Council – who were involved at the outset – and The Baring Foundation, The City of London, Trustee Savings Bank, and The Croydon Resource Centre Trust.

The Commission wishes to thank the Administrative Assistant, Maria Hartnett, for her able and dedicated work.

Finally, but above all, the Commission records its appreciation of the outstanding work of the Secretary, Frances Morrell, who made an exceptional commitment and contribution to all aspects of the Commission's work and in particular to the writing of this Report.

Summary of the Argument

The Speaker's Commission was established to look at ways in which citizens can participate fully and effectively in society.

The theme of this Report is the separate role of individuals as citizens within the political or public community, and the rules that govern it. We believe that citizenship is one of the most important concepts of modern political struggle and social development. We do not discuss wealth creation, the relationship between management, workers and consumers, and the rules of the economic community, vital though that subject is. Neither do we discuss rules, responsibilities and roles within the family. We have adopted as a yardstick for contemporary re-evaluation of citizenship an analysis which, so far as we can judge, corresponds to the perceptions of the British people today.

Our society is passing through a period of change and we are concerned that without our realising it, we could lose some of the benefits of living in the relatively free and open society which we have inherited. The status and entitlements of all individuals is affected by the United Kingdom's membership of the European Communities and changing relationship with the Commonwealth. Since the war, Britain has been transformed into a multi-racial society. At the same time, shifts in the income, life style, nature of work and demographic balance of the population are affecting people's expectations, traditional arrangements for working life, retirement and care in the community.

Furthermore, the individual's role as a consumer and the responsibility of Government to safeguard freedom of choice has been reasserted over the last decade. In parallel, the scope, role, finance, management and accountability of public services has been contested. Debate about these exceptional changes has not provoked a parallel concern with citizenship issues. It is as though the rights of individuals in this country are regarded as superior to the rights of those in other countries but best left unstated. The Commission does not take this view. Citizenship, whatever it means, is a cultural achievement, a gift of history, which can be lost or destroyed. The Commission's purpose in publishing this Report is to propose practical ways in which our participatory arrangements can be strengthened so that they remain efficient rather than simply dignified, or ceremonial, parts of the constitution.

The challenge to our society in the late twentieth century is to create conditions where all who wish can become actively involved, can understand and participate, can influence, persuade, campaign and whistleblow, and in the making of decisions can work together for the mutual good. We deliberately did not, therefore, confine our attention to formal structures alone, for civil, political and social entitlements and services are not delivered solely through official institutions. We considered the numerous forms of independent and voluntary contribution to society and its citizens, for they too play an important part.

Evidence brought to our attention showed that nearly half the public have engaged in some kind of fund raising and a quarter have cared for a dependent relative. Caring for and helping others, especially the growing percentage of elderly people in our society, many in impoverished circumstances, is something that about six million people do on a voluntary basis, many devoting much of their time to it. The Government has acknowledged that their total input is greater than the combined inputs financed from central and local government. We heard predictions of a twenty-five per cent rise in the number of pensioners in the near future, making the issue of opportunities for participation for all members of society, irrespective of age, and the question of caring even more vital.

Having considered the many factors described in the Report – our rapidly changing society, the entitlements of citizens in the late twentieth century, and the obligations of public institutions, of which many are ignorant; the plight of the sick, the elderly, and the handicapped; the contributions of the thousands of individuals who care for the environment or for their fellows on a voluntary or professional basis – we drew up a series of recommendations for action.

Our recommendations begin with matters such as how people may in the future learn more effectively what being a citizen actually means. We recognise the difficulty faced by teachers in schools trying to teach citizenship within the framework of a national curriculum which was originally conceived as a set of separate academic subjects, rather than as a collection of themes such as citizenship. We recommend that citizenship should, nevertheless, be a part of the education of every pupil from the early years right through to further and higher education; that children's achievement in this field should be recognised in their Record of Achievement and that consideration should be given to the most appropriate way of taking into account citizenship activities in applications for places in higher education.

Concerned that all citizens should be able to enjoy their full legal and social rights, we recommend two major reviews. Firstly, we propose a review and codification of the law relating to the legal rights, duties and entitlements of citizens in the United Kingdom.

Secondly, we propose a sector by sector review of the relationship between the statutory and voluntary bodies involved in public services which would define the frontier between them and their respective roles and responsibilities. We further suggest that a comprehensive citizens' advice and advocacy service should be provided.

Several of our recommendations refer to community activity and we advocate proper support for volunteers working from schooldays onwards, a modification of the present honours system to recognise citizenship and voluntary achievements, a review of the disincentives and obstacles to volunteering, including an encouragement to under-represented groups, and financial assistance to those volunteers who need it.

Finally, we recommend that employers should formulate policy guidelines, if they do not have them already, about their community involvement, that there should be a Parliamentary award to bodies making an outstanding contribution to the community, and that a national independent institution should be set up to support citizenship developments.

Recommendations

Learning to be a citizen

1. The Commission recommends that the study and experience of citizenship should be a part of every young person's education from the earliest years of schooling and continuing into the post-school years within further and higher education and the youth service, whether in state or private sector schools, and irrespective of the course of study being followed.

2. The Commission recommends, as does the Council of Europe, that the main international charters and conventions on human rights to which the UK is signatory should provide the reference points within the classroom for the study of citizenship.

3. The Commission recommends that every school governing body should request that a strategy should be developed and monitored for incorporating citizenship studies across the curriculum; and should consider a progress report regularly.

4. The Commission recommends that evidence of activities undertaken as part of learning citizenship skills across the curriculum should be included in a student's Record of Achievement.

5. The Commission recommends that schools and colleges should use the material in this report for curriculum and assessment purposes and that each of these institutions should hold a copy of the full report.

6. The Commission recommends that the study and promotion of citizenship in schools should be continued at Leicester University in partnership with Northamptonshire and Leicestershire County Councils.

7. The Commission recommends that institutions in the higher education sector should formulate explicit selection policies and consider how most appropriately to take into account evidence of a candidate's citizenship activities.

8. The Commission recommends that each local education authority reviews the range and type of support available for community work and citizenship activities, particularly within the youth service and adult education.

9. The Commission recommends that the judiciary, civil service, teachers, doctors and nurses, local government officers, the police and the armed forces should have specific training on the entitlements and duties of citizens and the corresponding obligations of public institutions as set out in documents such as the European Convention.

Citizenship and the administration of justice

10. The Commission recommends a review and codification of the law relating to the legal rights, duties and entitlements of the citizen in the United Kingdom and the dissemination of this information in a clear way to all citizens. We urge the Lord Chancellor to invite the Government and other appropriate individuals and institutions to consult on the best way of ensuring these objectives.

11. The Commission recommends that there should be a comprehensive citizens' advice service which would include a national advocacy scheme for those disadvantaged groups who cannot claim their own entitlements.

Public services and the voluntary sector

12. The Commission recommends that a floor of adequate social entitlements should be maintained, monitored and improved when possible by central government, with the aim of enabling every citizen to live the life of a civilised human being according to the standards prevailing in society.

13. The Commission recommends that central government should complement the investigations into the extent of volunteer activity and the work of the voluntary sector now being carried out by the Volunteer Centre and National Council of Voluntary Organisations (NCVO), by co-ordinating a public review, which would determine:
    (a) the boundaries between statutory and voluntary responsibilities in the public services on a sector by sector basis
    (b) the boundaries between the roles of professionals and auxiliary workers and those of volunteers in the publicly funded services
    (c) ways of ensuring efficient and effective use of public funds through a cost-benefit analysis of the potential contribution of volunteers to service agencies
    (d) guidelines for the involvement of under-represented groups
    (e) guidelines for the effective employment of volunteers in different settings.

Opportunities for volunteering

14. The Commission recommends:
     (a) the provision of a comprehensive, nationwide network of information, publicly available, to direct volunteers to where their skills can best be used
     (b) the involvement of public broadcasting in providing information about opportunities for volunteers and urges radio and television authorities to participate in this service
     (c) that volunteers carrying out tasks for local and central Government should receive reasonable expenses
     (d) the provision of structured state support for the training and management of volunteers who are involved with professionals in the delivery of social rights
     (e) that managing volunteers should be part of the training of appropriate professionals, such as social workers or teachers.

Parliament

15. The Commission recommends that Parliament considers how it can best through its own institutions ensure that the recommendations which relate to the responsibility of central government be effectively implemented and independently monitored. We have in mind particularly the proposals for the review and codification of the law, for the review of the boundaries between statutory and voluntary responsibilities and the proposals for developing a Parliamentary role in the honours system.

Public recognition

16. The Commission recommends that for as long as an honours system exists, a new part of the honours system should be developed which gives distinctive and equal weight to citizenship and voluntary achievements as it does at present to political, diplomatic, military, and civil service achievements.
     (a) A volunteer medal should be established and awarded to individuals and organisations who have given outstanding service to the community.
     (b) A Parliamentary award should be instituted to recognise those bodies which make outstanding contributions to the community.

Citizenship and public and private sector enterprises

17. The Commission recommends that all major enterprises should consider formulating corporate policy on community

involvement, along the lines currently being developed by the Industry and Parliament Trust model, and give greater publicity within their organisation and externally about their policies regarding existing corporate community involvement.

Conclusion

18. The Commission recommends the establishment of either a Standing Royal Commission on Citizenship, or an Organisation with a Royal Charter publishing an annual report, or an Independent Body with a Board of Trustees, to deal with all aspects of citizenship:

   - to document and research social, economic and educational aspects of citizenship;

   - to consider new legislation, in relation to the rights and duties of citizens;

   - to stimulate informed public discussion.

   The Commission urges the Speaker to pursue this proposal.

What Citizenship Means: The Commission's Starting Point

What Citizenship Means: The Commission's Starting Point

1. Introduction: The Difficulty of Defining Citizenship

We began by defining our own approach to citizenship. At a seminar, Members considered papers presented by Sir Ralf Dahrendorf, Professor Norman Barrie, Professor Raymond Plant, Roger Henderson Q.C. and Paul Boateng M.P.

We commissioned two separate pieces of research. The first, on the views of young people, by Ann Richardson of Social and Community Planning Research (SCPR), was commissioned by the Prince's Trust and the Commission (*Talking About Commitment*, 1990). The second, a national survey of schools, was conducted by Professor Fogelman of Leicester University and Social and Community Planning and Research. A paper setting out the Commission's approach was circulated widely on a consultative basis. The Commission drew at a later stage on a wide range of academic work, published and unpublished.

An immediate difficulty facing us is that in our society the term 'citizenship' is an unfamiliar notion. Asked about it, young people 'almost invariably found themselves with a moment or more of embarrassed silence . . . the fact that the word 'citizenship' is not in common use was frequently commented upon' (Richardson 1990, 8).

Political philosophers suggested to the Commission that agreement on the meaning of citizenship in principle is very difficult.

> Trying to pin down *the* definition as the only true or real one is in itself a political activity because it brings into play a more general normative or ideological commitment within which an idea of citizenship sits as a part. (Plant, Commission on Citizenship 1989, 1)

Other thinkers argued that democracy itself is a sham. Citizens' actions, struggles and movements are assumed 'to reveal their impotence, dependency, and in any case their ignorance in respect of the powers of such phenomena as the state's bureaucracy, the ruling groups and elites, dominant and mystifying ideologies and ultimately socio-economic forces' (Roche 1987, 363).

Our research into the teaching of citizenship in schools established that, although many schools claimed to address the subject, there was 'an extraordinary multiplicity of interpretations of its meaning' (Fogelman 1990, 5). We were interested in the divisions among political philosophers and the relative lack of interest until recently on the part of academic theorists, in contrast to the deep concern of citizens themselves, in the nature of citizenship, citizen politics and citizen communities. Young people felt indignant at the failure to teach them about their citizenship, and what it meant for them.

> It is unusual to find wide consensus on any issue. Yet in this study, there was one issue which united virtually everyone across the social spectrum. From those who had left school with few qualifications to those in university or beyond, there was a strong call for more teaching of the issues surrounding citizenship in schools . . . One 17 year old put the argument this way: 'You should know about it – it's your life, it's your community – and you really have a responsibility to yourself to know about it'. (Richardson 1990, 35)

2. Towards a Definition

We were aware of the long tradition of Western thought about citizenship, from Aristotle's *Politics* – 'A citizen is one who has a share in both ruling and being ruled. Deliberative or judicial, we deem him to be a citizen' – to the writings of Cicero, Machiavelli, Burke, de Tocqueville, Mill, and, in our own century, Hannah Arendt.

We considered that, for this country, any definition we adopted had to include legal membership of a political community based on universal suffrage, and also membership of a civil community based on the rule of law. The definition, framework, and approach to be found in the work of T. H. Marshall, whose classic theory was first published in 1950, seemed to us to provide a sensible starting point.

Marshall's definition itself is an open one: it recognises citizenship as a process. Marshall includes in his definition a social element, and in doing so seems to reflect the British approach to citizenship. According to Marshall citizenship is:

> a status bestowed on all those who are full members of a community. All who possess the status are equal with respect to the rights and duties with which that status is endowed. There is no universal

principle that determines what those rights and duties shall be, but societies in which citizenship is a developing institution create an image of an ideal citizenship against which achievement can be directed . . . The urge forward along the path thus plotted is an urge towards a fuller measure of equality, an enrichment of the stuff of which the status is made and an increase in the number of those on whom the status is bestowed . . . Citizenship requires a . . . direct sense of community membership based on loyalty to a civilisation which is a common possession. It is a loyalty of free men endowed with rights and protected by a common law. Its growth is stimulated both by the struggle to win those rights and by their enjoyment when won. (Marshall 1950, 28–9 & 40–1)

Marshall envisaged citizenship as involving three elements, civil, political and social, which he argued were developed in successive centuries: civil rights in the eighteenth, political in the nineteenth and social in the twentieth.

The civil element is composed of the rights necessary for individual freedom – liberty of the person, freedom of speech, thought and faith, the right to own property and to conclude valid contracts, and the right to justice. The last is of a different order from the others because it is the right to defend and assert all one's rights on terms of equality with others and by due process of law. This shows us that the institutions most directly associated with civil rights are the courts of justice.

By the political element I mean the right to participate in the exercise of political power, as a member of a body invested with political authority or as an elector of the members of such a body. The corresponding institutions are Parliament and councils of local government.

By the social element I mean the whole range from the right to a modicum of economic welfare and security to the right to share to the full in the social heritage and to live the life of a civilised being according to the standards prevailing in the society. The institutions most closely connected with it are the education system and the social services. (Marshall 1950, 10–11)

How people define citizenship

In working with our partners on new initiatives, we have checked whether or not Marshall's approach represents their understanding of citizenship.

Our own consultative conference on citizenship in schools supported Marshall's definition, subject to updating the language. We noted that the quantitative research carried out by Richardson and Crewe was also consistent with Marshall's approach to the social dimension of citizenship.

For young adults, being a citizen meant belonging, either as a result of nationality or through conforming to the laws and coming to be accepted – that is, by virtue of domicile. It involved rights such as 'the right to express your views without being in jail or shot'. Limits were set on the power of those in authority: 'They can't just chuck you in prison and forget about you ... They can only hold you for so long'. It also involved duties 'to pay taxes and abide by the law' (Richardson 1990, 8).

Adults took a similarly phrased view of rights: 'the right not to be murdered'; 'the right not to be molested'; 'the right to expect others to be law-abiding' (Johnston Conover et al 1990, 13).

When asked directly what were the most important rights 'the majority of British citizens had no hesitation in according primacy to social rights ... to a minimum standard of living, to medical care, to a job, and to education' (Johnston Conover et al 1990, 13).

Those consulted agreed that 'rights are not universal, but instead depend on the country and the historical period in which one lives'. They are won by struggle, 'we are going back to the rights of every century when people have fought and died to give us our rights in this century' (Johnston Conover et al 1990, 18).

On responsibilities, the views of the British citizen were clear: 'Far and away the most commonly cited British duty, however, was obedience to the law ... combined with a more general emphasis on civility or obedience to community norms' (Johnston Conover et al 1990, 21).

3. Rights, Duties and Obligations: The Commission's Perspective

We have set out a traditional British analysis of citizenship which, so far as we can judge, seems to match British people's perceptions of it. Certain terms in regular use in the discussion of citizenship are regularly disputed. We felt we should make clear what we mean by rights, duties and obligations.

Rights

- *Rights are a set of entitlements.* They are a very precise concept, 'not one of moral exhortation but one of the realities of people's lives'. (Dahrendorf, Commission on Citizenship, 2)

- *Rights are necessarily individual.* 'Although a limited company or a charitable foundation, such as your sponsors, can epitomise and espouse the characteristics of citizenship, neither can enjoy citizenship. Only a single human being can claim whatever it is that is citizenship.' (Henderson, unpublished paper, 2)

- *Rights are residual entitlements.* There is no accessible, comprehensive statement of the rights of citizens in the UK, such as is found in the constitutions of other countries. The foundation of government in the UK is the notion that Parliament is the supreme authority, and that the validity of its legislation cannot therefore be challenged in the UK courts. As a result, the individual's freedoms are residual: that is, they exist to the extent that Parliament has not enacted restrictions, and they are vulnerable to any subsequent enactment of Parliament.

- *Rights include social rights.* Supporters of the classical liberal perspective reject the concept of social rights because it undermines the market and the open society within which it is possible for individuals with differing ends and purposes to live together.

We support the analysis put to us by Dahrendorf: 'From an early point onwards in our century, more and more people came to believe that civil and political rights are not worth an awful lot unless they are backed up by a certain basic social security which enables people to make use of these rights and makes it impossible for others to push them around in such a way that the rights become an empty constitutional promise without any substance . . . a floor on which everyone stands and below which no-one must fall.' (Dahrendorf, Commission on Citizenship, 4)

Duties

As we have said, in the UK there is no comprehensive constitutional list of entitlements. Individuals' freedoms exist to the extent that Parliament has not enacted restrictions. By the same token, there is no list of duties. However, citizens have a duty to respect the law. The duty to pay taxes, to serve on juries or to refrain from treasonable activities are examples of what is required of a citizen on this basis.

We do not accept that there is a simple quid pro quo relationship – a bargain – between entitlements and duties for each individual citizen. This key issue was highlighted by a number of speakers. We agree with Dahrendorf . 'There are rights of citizenship and there are [duties]. Both are absolutely valid if they are valid at all, but we shouldn't turn them into a quid pro quo' (Dahrendorf, Commission on Citizenship, 6). In other words, both exist in their own right; the relationship between them is far from simple.

Obligations

It is useful to distinguish between the entitlements and duties of citizenship, and the obligations of institutions funded by the taxpayer which exist, in part, to give effect to the entitlements. Three sets of institutions – the Courts, Parliament and Local Councils, and the institutions of the education and social services – correspond respectively to the three kinds of entitlements: civil, political and social. Clearly, entitlements would not exist without institutions charged with the responsibility of giving them effect.

In considering citizenship, therefore, the Commission means to consider in the first place the relationship between the entitlements and duties of the individual on the one hand and the corresponding obligations of public institutions on the other, as well as the framework of rules to which they both conform. We must add that we do not believe that the whole exercise by citizens of their civil, political and social entitlements is contained within that formal structure, as the traditional analysis seems to suggest.

4. The Public Good

The voluntary contribution by individual citizens to the common good through the participation in and exercise of civic duty and the encouragement of such activities by public and private institutions is a part of citizenship. Decentralised local administration and a variety of active organisations and opportunities for individual involvement are the key to democracy. Free associations, free trade unions and democratically elected local government represent collective rights held in common. Within the public or political community individuals consult and argue, listen and persuade and in so doing, accept the idea of a public good that transcends the private.

Carole Pateman, a leading writer on this theme, envisages a political community as a political association of a multiplicity of political associations. The members of the community are 'citizens in many . . . associations which are bound together through horizontal and multi-faceted tiers of self assumed political obligation. The essential feature . . . is that the political sphere is one dimension, the collective dimension of social life as a whole. It is the area of social existence in which citizens voluntarily co-operate together and sustain their common life and common undertaking' (Pateman 1979, 174).

SECTION II

Impediments to Citizenship

Impediments to Citizenship

1. Introduction

The Commission took the post-war British description of citizenship, set out in Section I, as a yardstick, and looked at the contemporary relationship betwen citizens and public institutions. We asked whether there were major impediments existing in those formal arrangements which hindered the citizen's ability to participate.

In particular, we asked whether citizens – and those placed in authority over them – knew and understood the individual's entitlements and duties, and the obligations of the citizenship institutions; in other words, whether there was a shared understanding of the guiding principles of our democracy.

We asked whether it was clear who was, or who was not, a member of the legally constituted community of the United Kingdom, and whether those who enjoyed the status of citizen were in an equal position with regard to their entitlements and duties. Finally, we asked whether individuals had access to their rights and how far social disadvantage remained an impediment.

In order to help us, we commissioned a paper from Piers Gardner of the British Institute of International and Comparative Law. A seminar was held at the Institute on that paper. We drew on the series of surveys of schools, employers and selectors for Higher Education that we had commissioned. We held a major consultative conference at Northampton, attended by 700 people, and a series of small seminars. We considered evidence tabled by Commission Members, such as the United Nations Report on Human Development.

2. Belonging to a Community and Knowing the Rules

Being a citizen involves, according to Marshall, 'belonging to a community', but he suggests that there are no 'universal principles' that determine what that entails. The legally defined national community is the most easily recognised society within which

11

citizenship rights and duties exist. A British citizen is a member of a legally defined national community, and should, in consequence of a long period of evolution, enjoy civil, political and social entitlements and duties that go with the status. Secondly, such entitlements and duties extend beyond national frontiers as the result of national membership of broader groups, for example, the European Communities. Finally, we can speak of membership of a world community, with rights in international law established in the post-war period.

We agree that there are no 'universal principles' analagous to the laws of science that determine what the status of membership of a community entails. In this context, we considered two points. In the Commission's view, one of the most important aspects of citizenship is that it involves the maintenance of an agreed framework of rules governing the relationships of individuals to the State and to one another. Secondly, each of those communities has developed a set of rules, valid in law.

During the post-war period, the UK has agreed a number of Declarations and Conventions. These set out our principles on human rights, so far as the world community is concerned, and also in relation to the European Community. All domestic political parties, for many decades, have accepted the UK's position with regard to these Conventions. Indeed, the UK played a leading role in developing them: for example, as a drafting member of the Council of Europe which elaborated the European Convention on Human Rights, and the first state to ratify the Convention.

The Universal Declaration of Human Rights was adopted by the United Nations in December 1948. The Declaration was the inspiration behind later multilateral human rights conventions and the inclusion in constitutions of newly emerged States of human rights guarantees. The European Convention on Human Rights came into force on 3 September 1953. These texts marked an alteration in the status of the individual in international law, recognising the entitlements of individuals – their human rights – irrespective of their citizenship of a particular state; this so-called 'new citizenship' is discussed in Appendix D.

The European Social Charter, which is the counterpart of the European Convention on Human Rights in the sphere of economic and social rights, was signed at Turin on 18 October 1961, and entered into force on 26 February 1965. The supervisory system under the Charter differs in important respects from that of the European Convention. The Charter makes no provision for binding decisions by judicial or quasi-judicial means. Individuals have no right of direct petition. However, both the Charter and the Convention recognise rights vested in the individual and not tied to the existence of any national affiliation.

The underlying principles of our own system of entitlements and duties, and obligations of citizenship institutions, are similar to those outlined in the conventions. For example, the rights to education and health treatment are based on residence rather than on nationality. European Community nationals have rights of movement and entitlements to social security benefits which are, to an extent, attached to the individual. Accrued benefits can thus be retained when the individual moves from one Member State to another.

Plainly the relationship between laws, rules, traditions and conventions is complicated. Terms such as human rights and citizenship entitlements overlap, but do not have the same meaning. A technical review is outside the scope of this Report. We would make the simple point that many individuals in the UK play an active role, through travel, work, leisure or community activity, in more than one legally defined community.

The importance of rules

We consider that citizenship involves the perception and maintenance of an agreed framework of rules or guiding principles, rather than shared values.

Such a framework of rules is more than a set of external texts whose legitimacy is acknowledged: an agreed framework of rules provides the shared basis whereby individuals relate day to day to the 'fellow strangers' of their community; 'there are more citizens in a nation state than any individual could meet, let alone get to know well in a life-time. They are not complete strangers however – as in the case of people from entirely different places and cultures . . . they are a community of fellow strangers' (Roche 1987, 376).

3. Lack of Knowledge

Belonging to a community involves at a minimum an understanding of the framework of rules or guiding principles that govern that community. Lack of knowledge is a serious impediment to full citizenship. The qualitative investigations carried out by Richardson and others showed that British citizens lacked a clear understanding of these matters.

While understanding is transmitted in the first instance through the family, it plainly falls to the schools to teach citizenship during the planned, compulsory, educational experience of the child, from five to sixteen years of age. The Council of Europe has declared that 'throughout their school career all young people should learn about human rights as part of their preparation for life in a pluralistic democracy' (Council of Europe 1985, 1). We decided to investigate the contributions of British schools. Our research revealed that there was no systematic teaching of citizenship in the UK.

In September of 1989, a survey was conducted for the Commission by Leicester University and Social and Community Planning Research (SCPR), to find out how citizenship was taught in schools. The survey covered teaching on subjects, topics and issues concerned with citizenship and the community, student participation in the decision making structure within the school, and involvement through the school in community activity. Eight hundred schools were surveyed: nearly two thirds of the schools responded to the survey, which indicates the high level of interest and enthusiasm for the subject within many schools. Some insight into the importance which a school places on this area of the curriculum can be inferred from how it is treated within the policy and management structures of the school. Nearly half (forty three per cent) of schools reported that they had an agreed policy, curriculum document or written statement about citizenship studies within the school, although for only 5 per cent was this a separate document rather than part of a wider curriculum document. A complementary in depth survey was conducted by Northamptonshire and Leicestershire County Councils, under the direction of Professor Fogelman.

In the Commission's view the most telling finding is the range of topics included in citizenship studies. Schools were asked to indicate, separately for each year group, which specific topics falling within their definition of citizenship/community studies were taught in the past year. The range of replies was far too great to make any systematic summary, but some examples may help to give a flavour of the great variety of topics which are relevant to citizenship being covered by schools.

For twelve to thirteen year olds, they included:

> nature conservation; charity involvement; pollution; the Christian Community; support for the third world; health and safety; the family; relationships; making choices; voting and the parliamentary system; police and policing; the aged; alcohol education; eating for health; recreation; smoking; skills for adolescence; people who serve our community; third world communities; personal safety; decision making; lifestyles; money management. (Fogelman 1990, 6)

For fifteen to sixteen year olds:

> world of work; health; morals; conflict and reconciliation in the community; national and international affairs; trades unions; duties

and rights of adults; family responsibility; social awareness; the media; the school and the community; mental health studies; sexual relationships and decision making; persecution and prejudice; using local agencies; body abuse; local government; parliament; child care; crime and crime prevention; consumer awareness; population growth; care of elderly people; handicap in the community; respect for the environment; child development; youth cultures. (Fogelman 1990, 6)

Many topics were taught and the amount of time devoted to citizenship as a whole varied substantially.

We found it interesting to compare the arrangements, revealed in the Commission surveys, for fostering a young person's sense of citizenship, with the approach recommended by the Committee of Ministers of the Council of Europe, in a recommendation adopted on 14 May 1985.

Conscious of the need to reaffirm democratic values in the face of:
– intolerance, acts of violence, terrorism;
– the re-emergence of the public expression of racist and xenophobic attitudes;
– the disillusionment of many young people in Europe who are affected by the economic recession and aware of the continuing poverty and inequality in the world;
  Believing therefore that throughout their school career, all young people should learn about human rights as part of their preparation for life in a pluralistic democracy;
  Convinced that schools are communities which can and should be an example of the dignity of the individual and for difference, for tolerance and for equality of opportunity;
  Recommends that the governments of member states . . . encourage teaching and learning about human rights in school. (Council of Europe 1985, 1)

The text sets out the skills and knowledge to be acquired from an early age and the contribution of the climate of the school and its relationship to the community.

In March 1990, six months after our survey, the National Curriculum Council produced the third document in its Curriculum Guidance series, entitled *The Whole Curriculum*. In this document, five themes were identified by the NCC as seeming ' . . . to most people pre-eminent. It is reasonable to assume at this stage that they are essential parts of the whole curriculum.' One of these themes is identified as being Education for Citizenship.

We welcomed this initiative for which we had pressed. However, we recognised that much will have to be done if human rights and citizenship as a theme is to be translated into an educational reality for students in British schools. Furthermore, opportunities for learning to be a citizen should, we believe, continue after statutory schooling. We return to that theme on page 38. The Commission also concluded that the agreed rules should be understood not only by young people and their teachers, but generally among the adult population, particularly among those who exercise authority over their fellow citizens. This raises questions of training, which we discuss on page 41.

4. Legal Confusion

We also considered whether citizens had access to their rights in law. Citizenship is the attribute of individuals as members of a political body; the rules that establish that body are legal ones. The Commission asked Piers Gardner, Director of the British Institute of International and Comparative Law, to advise them on the definition of community in legal terms, and to explain who was, and who was not, a member. It appears that the legal status of individuals in the United Kingdom is complicated.

The British Nationality Act (1981) defines a British citizen, and certain other statutes such as the Representation of the People Act (1983) refer back to this definition in conferring the right to vote or stand for election or other enabling provisions. On the one hand, non-citizens can exercise what we would normally believe to be key aspects of the formal relationship between individuals and the State, such as voting, which do not depend on holding United Kingdom citizenship. Commonwealth citizens may vote in the UK, for example, as may citizens of the Irish Republic. On the other hand, the right of residence – often regarded as an attribute of citizenship based on nationality – is not enjoyed by a significant number of individuals whose nationality status depends on, or is regulated by, the British Nationality Act of 1981.

The United Kingdom definition of nationality creates classes of citizenship. The opportunity for citizens to participate in the political process depends on another attribute of the individual, namely residence. This attribute is a right for some classes of citizen but not for all.

Another anomaly is the fact that the European Communities Act (1972) asserted the supremacy of European Community Law over the law of England, Wales, Scotland and Ireland. Under European Community law as implemented by that Act, workers from other Community countries enjoy freedom of movement to seek jobs and establish businesses here, but the right to reside and work does not include political rights. This is in keeping with the European Community's essentially economic role.

16

The position is made more complicated still when the new citizenship rights, protected by the European Convention, are considered. Like the Scandinavian countries, the United Kingdom has not included the convention in national law. It has, however, granted the right to individuals directly to petition the European Commission of Human Rights where they allege a breach of the Convention. Hence in a number of cases the Human Rights institutions in Strasbourg have had to consider arguments about these questions, which British courts have not been able to consider. Where the United Kingdom has been found to have violated the Convention, domestic law has been amended to prevent recurrence, adding to the confusing patchwork of legal provision affecting the relationship between the citizen and the state. Workers moving to the United Kingdom from other Community countries in the future may well feel that their citizenship rights are less clearly protected in the United Kingdom than in the other Community countries. Most of these countries have either incorporated the Convention or have a national written code of human rights. The United Kingdom has neither. Our law deals with these questions in a piecemeal way.

The legal relationship between individuals and the State has a social dimension. The right to education, for example, and adequate health treatment are provided for in the new citizenship (referred to on page 12) as well as the right to free speech and other civil rights.

Citizenship appears to exist concurrently on three levels: the limited level of legal nationality; the level of entitlements stemming from residence in an area, which accrue regardless of nationality; and the level of human rights guaranteed to all individuals irrespective of their nationality or residence status.

The Commission concluded that membership of a political community in the UK and the related question of entitlements and responsibilities is confusing.

Civil rights

The confusion over who is, or who is not, a member of the political community, creates problems of access to civil and to social rights: other difficulties of access may compound the problem.

The United Kingdom has traditionally protected the individual against the State. This may be illustrated by the early ratification of the European Convention on Human Rights and the Social Charter (1961), with the specific legal obligations which both impose. However, for historical reasons set out in Appendix D, the legal framework governing the relationship between those who are legally members of the political community and the State is obscure, confusing and therefore excessively reliant on the advice of specialist lawyers and cumbersome and costly court proceedings.

> The test of accessibility of the law is not, therefore, whether a specialist lawyer can advise on the question with accuracy. It is whether the individual who needs to rely upon the protection or benefit which the law provides can understand it. Democratic participation requires that the law should be simple and accessible: that people should know where they stand. (Gardner, 6)

Although the UK has ' . . . a Rolls-Royce system, it is a thoroughly defective system in that it wholly fails at the moment to deal with a vast area of necessary advice on the rights of the citizen' (Henderson, unpublished, 9). Legal complexity divides citizens from their rights, and this is accentuated by the cost. Henderson asks how such a vast gap actually affects the citizen. The Commission agrees with his conclusion. Such inaccessibility is more than an impediment to citizenship: it is a fundamental denial.

The development of the European Community can be expected, at least initially, to accentuate the difficulties with this legal patchwork. For example, Community Law already requires equality of treatment between men and women as regards social security benefits. This requirement provides the basis of a legal challenge by an individual where national provisions fail to achieve such equality. But this is a provision in the UK which is superimposed on the existing law; an added dimension which may not always be easy to recognise.

The Commission concludes that a review and codification of the law relating to the legal rights, duties and entitlements of the citizen and the obligations of citizenship is urgently needed.

5. Obstacles to Participation

The right to participate in the exercise of political power, as a member of a body invested with political authority or as an elector of the members of such a body is a central entitlement of each citizen in a democracy. As the Commission has pointed out, the exercise of such rights is tied up with the question of legal membership of the political community described above. Further impediments exist.

Parliament, local councils, the magistracy, the trusts of voluntary bodies, school governing bodies, the lay councils of trade unions, local chambers of commerce and a great range of other bodies represent valuable opportunities for citizens to be involved in public policy making and decision making. A recent Report of the Hansard Society Commission on 'Women at the Top', chaired by Lady Howe, drew attention to the serious under-representation of women in Parliament, in public bodies, in recognition in the honours system, on Boards and Trades Unions Executives. The Commission drew attention to the reduction by central Government in the budget of the Equal Opportunities Commission and called for a Speaker's Conference to consider ways in which parliamentary and party practices and procedures place women at a real disadvantage.

An HMSO publication *The Local Government Councillor* (1986) threw an interesting light on the characteristics of councillors. In 1985 less than 20 per cent of councillors were women, though women make up 51 per cent of the whole population. The percentage of owner occupiers in the whole population is increasing, but at a faster rate amongst councillors so that in 1985, 85 per cent of councillors were owner occupiers while only 57 per cent of the whole population fell into this category. Twenty five per cent of councillors had a degree, as compared with 5 per cent of the population. Forty one per cent of councillors either currently worked, or worked pre-retirement, in the kind of professional or management positions held by 14 per cent of the whole population. Only 5 per cent of councillors worked, or used to work, in semi-skilled or unskilled manual occupations, as compared to 25 per cent in the general population.

Our system of justice depends heavily on lay involvement, whether it be trial by jury or trial by a lay bench. The appointment of Justices of the Peace enables the ordinary man or woman to contribute to the way in which society deals with juveniles in trouble, with adult offenders, and with men, women and children caught up in domestic problems. Real difficulties exist in recruiting suitable persons for the magistracy and their retention following appointment. So far as magistrates are concerned such evidence as is available points to a disproportionate social balance among the magistracy. It is broadly middle class but it should represent the social balance of society more closely. The Lord Chancellor's Department is endeavouring to bring onto the bench candidates from all walks of life. However, the very low number of magistrates from the ethnic minority communities is a matter for concern. The years since 1985 have shown that more suitable candidates are coming forward. The percentage appointed was 4.07 in 1985, 4.57 in 1986 and since then it has exceeded at about 6 per cent the percentage in the total population in the age range 35 to 54. The particular difficulties facing older people are discussed on pages 32–3.

No comparable information is available on the membership of Trusts. School governing bodies have just been reconstituted. The Scottish Consumer Council Report 'Can Anyone Get On These?' offers a helpful initiative for the future. Overall it seems a substantial effort is needed if access to lay bodies is to be genuinely open to all candidates.

The Commission identified a further issue. The democratic framework, implied in Marshall's description of political rights, would be regarded by many as limited. Essentially it supposes that citizens, having chosen their national and local representative by ballot, have exercised their political rights to the full and will not participate further in decision making within their society. Civil rights are safeguarded. Social rights are settled by the same process and will be delivered by professionally managed public services accountable to those the citizen has elected. In the Commission's view, this is not an accurate picture of life in contemporary Britain. The question is discussed in Section III.

6. Social Disadvantage

In considering social rights, as described by Marshall, the Commission considered the Human Development Report (1990) published by the United Nations. The Human Development Index set out in the Report measures human development, not by the yardstick of income alone, but by a more comprehensive index reflecting life expectancy, literacy, and command over resources to enjoy a decent standard of living.

In an index which ranges from low to high human development over 130 countries, the United Kingdom ranks a high 121. Only the Scandinavian countries, Japan, Netherlands, Canada, Australia and France are higher. In terms of GNP per head, the United Kingdom is ranked lower, at 113. The Report shows that for British citizens, the post-war trend has been favourable in terms of life expectancy, infant mortality, calorie supply and per capita income, though a widening of income differentials has been recorded recently. The Commission accepts the implication of this Report that these findings show the fundamental importance to human development of key public services. In this context, the Commission welcomes the commitment made by all political parties to the maintenance of public services.

A floor of entitlements

Adam Smith in the eighteenth century defined the necessities of life:

> By necessaries I understand not only the commodities which are indispensibly necessary for the support of life, but what ever the custom of the country renders it indecent for creditable people, even the lowest order, to be without. A linen shirt, for example, is, strictly speaking, not a necessary of life. The Greeks and the Romans lived, I suppose, very comfortably though they had no linen. But in the

present times, through the greater part of Europe, a creditable day-labourer would be ashamed to appear in public without a linen shirt, the want of which would be supposed to denote that disgraceful degree of poverty which, it is presumed, nobody can well fall into without extreme bad conduct. Custom, in the same manner, has rendered leather shoes a necessary of life in England. The poorest creditable person of either sex would be ashamed to appear in public without them. (Adam Smith, 351–2)

Judged by Adam Smith's definition, a significant proportion of the population of the UK is poor. Many of these are disabled or disadvantaged for a range of other reasons. Among them are those who are so severely disadvantaged that their commitment can only be to their immediate day to day lives.

Poverty, bad housing, unemployment, religious, racial and sexual discrimination, physical and mental disability and ill-health, as well as the need to care for dependent members of the family, interact with one another to disadvantage a significant part of the population and prevent them from participating in ways that others take for granted. Those who are homeless and subject to vagrancy laws are by definition unable to exercise citizenship rights. They are, for example, unable to register to vote. Voluntary care for the elderly, mentally ill and mentally handicapped is increasing rapidly, in response both to demographic change and medical advances, and to community care policies. It is not always willingly undertaken. It often represents a very considerable restriction of citizenship.

The Commission considers that it is the duty of Government to enable people to have an equal opportunity to participate in citizenship. The duty includes the provision of a floor of social entitlements.

7. Administrative Complexity

How social entitlements are administered is an important practical citizenship issue. There is extensive evidence that many people who are eligible for benefits do not in fact claim them, particularly when they are means tested (Hill, 1990). There are many reasons for this that have been identified, including complexity of the regulations, the administrative hassle involved, stigma and other negative consequences or lack of real gains for the recipient. Clearly, knowledge of the entitlement is a pre-requisite for claiming it. Non take-up is particularly prevalent among people with a mental handicap.

For those living in poverty, the complexity of the benefits system is quite unacceptable. There is no easy way for citizens to discover their entitlements, or calculate whether they are worse or better off by claiming them. This is demonstrated by the fact that welfare rights specialists have to be employed as the field is too complicated for the average social worker to keep up to date. The access of the disadvantaged to social provision and entitlements itself becomes more complex. Professor Ruth Lister draws attention to one aspect of this problem. 'Inadequate and diminishing rights of social citizenship make it harder for poor people to exercise their rights of legal citizenship. Restrictions on the exercise of legal citizenship rights in the sphere of the welfare state undermine poor people's rights of social citizenship' (Lister 1990, 40).

8. Public Service Accountability

The managerial approach of the public services has often meant that the entitlements and duties of the individual and the specific obligations of the public bodies were rarely clear. Such an approach also discounted the contribution that communities can and need to make to the effectiveness of services.

Public education provides an example. Though standards have been raised overall, a recent survey by the Adult Literacy and Basic Skills Unit (1990) suggests that nearly one million people aged between 16 and 20 find it difficult to read and nearly 1.5 million have problems with spelling. About 300,000 adults are completely illiterate. Children of low income parents continue to have much lower chances of achieving qualifications than those of higher income parents. It is not easy to see how the notion of entitlements of the citizen or the obligations of the schools applied in these circumstances.

9. Conclusion

We began by comparing the system of citizenship in Britain as it was described in 1949 with present day arrangements. The broad structure remains the same but lack of knowledge, legal confusion, obstacles to public office, unduly complex social legislation and lack of clarity about entitlements, duties and obligations of public institutions are key impediments for British citizens today. Our recommendations on education and the administration of justice reflect our concern about these impediments.

SECTION III

Encouraging Citizenship

SECTION III

Encouraging Citizenship

1. Introduction

At the time when Marshall was preparing his analysis of citizenship, many expected independent associations to diminish in number with the establishment of the Welfare State. The reverse was the case:

> Taken together, the independent associations are growing numerically. Yet the extension of governmental administration to many social services formerly provided by the associations might seem to indicate that their importance to a democratic community was dwindling. It may be that they are expanding because being spontaneous, informal and autonomous, they are felt to be a refuge from the growing omnicompetence of government. (Political and Economic Planning 1947, 9)

Today institutions responsible for delivering citizenship entitlements are increasingly supported in the discharge of those responsibilities by a network of agencies, voluntary bodies, and volunteer effort.

In principle, the Commission supports a plural, participatory society.

> A variety of active organisations are the key to . . . democracy. Through active involvement in common concerns, the citizen can overcome the sense of relative isolation, and powerlessness that results from the insecurity of life in an increasingly commercial society. Associations along with decentralised local administration, mediate between the individual and the centralised state, providing forums in which opinion can be publicly and intelligently shaped, and the subtle habits of public initiative and responsibility learned and passed on. Associational life, in Tocqueville's thinking, is the best bulwark against the condition he feared most: the mass society of mutually antagonistic individuals, easy prey to despotism. These intermediate structures check, and restrain the tendencies of centralised government to assume more and more administrative control. (Bellah et al 1985, 38)

Our support is tempered by a concern that the balance of activity between the public and the voluntary should be appropriate. We decided first to assess the patterns of participatory activity that prevail today, before considering the practical ways in which citizens might be encouraged to participate. To help us in our work we commissioned a review of research evidence on voluntary activity from Janet Edwards of Leicester University, and a review of research evidence on active citizenship and a healthy society from David Halpern of St John's College, Cambridge. We also drew on a number of important reports published during the Commission's period of work.

2. Changes in the Pattern of Participation

People contribute voluntarily in a range of ways

Fund raising, according to a recent Volunteer Centre Survey, was the most common type of voluntary activity. Nearly half the public (47 per cent) had done this, followed by a third who had helped organise activities or events (31 per cent) and a quarter who had cared for a dependent relative (24 per cent).

> Four in ten of those who have been volunteers in the past six months have been involved in looking after the elderly (43 per cent). Around a quarter of recent volunteers have educated young people or helped physically handicapped people (27 per cent and 24 per cent respectively). Seventeen per cent have cared for the mentally handicapped. (MORI 1990, 13)

People may be contributing through voluntary organisations rather than political parties

A comparison of individual involvement in political parties, and with voluntary organisations was made recently by Christopher Patten MP, Secretary of State for the Environment, which indicated that people were increasingly involving themselves in independent bodies rather than political parties.

He compared party membership figures with those for voluntary organisations, 'making allowances for double counting, exaggeration and the large numbers of people who belong both to political parties and several non-governmental organisations' (Patten 1990, 6). He suggested that in 1980, individual membership of the Labour Party stood at 348,000. This figure fell to 250,000 in mid-decade, but after a recruitment campaign, is now said to be back at about 300,000. Membership of the Conservative Party reached a peak of just below 3 million in 1953. Throughout the 1980s it has allegedly stood at just above one third of that figure. [The Liberal Democrats currently claim 80,000 members].

He suggested that many charities have become effectively multi-million pound corporations, with larger annual budgets than those of political parties. The growth in membership of environmental groups was identified as especially striking. 'Friends of the Earth has grown from 25,000 members in 1980 to around 140,000 now. Greenpeace has rocketed from 30,000 in 1985 to over ten times that today. The National Trust has doubled its membership in 10 years from 950,000 to 1.9 million. You may say that these are high profile organisations, likely to attract new members in such numbers. But membership of the lesser-known Royal Society for Nature Conservation has grown by over 50 per cent, from under 140,000 to around 215,000 during the past decade. The pattern is the same right across the board' (Patten 1990, 6).

While accepting this shift, we recognise that political parties remain hugely influential. The organisational side of political parties provides a diverse set of career paths and those who choose this avenue often end up very close to the seats of power. Similarly, those who choose to seek office can rise to positions of very considerable power in local government and national government. Their problem is seldom lack of opportunity; the constraint is more likely to be financial, in that to run a major local authority committee takes so much time that to combine it with a lucrative job is difficult. Because of the general ignorance of the political system amongst school children in Britain, the scope for exerting influence through party politics is little understood. This is an important failure of our present education in citizenship. The Commission believes that schools should make better known the workings of the political system, and its accessibility.

People's perception of community has changed

We recognise that the word 'community' is difficult to define. It 'encourages skilful jumps from one meaning to another . . . Those advocating a new initiative, or those attacking or defending a particular point of view, may invoke the community in support of their case without making it clear which community they mean or in what sense they refer to it, or how far they have established what its opinions or interests are' (Willmott 1989, 5).

The nature of communities and people's involvement with them is predicted by the Henley Centre to be likely to change (*Planning for Social Change*, quoted in Edwards 1990). In discussing the use of the word 'community' the report comments on the wide range of contexts in which the word is found: 'community policing', 'the lesbian community', 'the European community' and 'the community charge' (Edwards 1990, 63).

It indicates that 'tightly knit geographically-based communities, as have been traditionally described, are becoming increasingly rare as the benefits of them to individuals fail, while the costs rise' (Edwards 1990, 64). While it seems inevitable that these communities 'will continue to decline', evidence suggests the growth of other forms of community in the 1990s. Membership of local groups is declining, but not of national ones. People may feel they have little in common with their neighbours and are less inclined to join a group which is local and territorially based such as in a city or neighbourhood, but are more likely to join one which is non-local and/or interest-based such as Friends of the Earth or a football supporters' club. But local territorial communities do remain and certain social trends are working in their favour in the 1990s; for example, greater numbers of people working from home and continued urbanisation.

We agree with *Planning for Social Change* that people involve themselves as individuals in an ever-growing and widening range of 'communities'. Environmentalism can be regarded as symbolic of the new relationship between individualism and collectivism – a balance between social responsibility for the environment and personal awareness of our relationship to that environment. There may be a continued decline in organised institutional collectives, but there is likely to be a growth in pressure groups concerned with a specific issue either with a wide remit like environmentalism or concentrating on one issue like banning cars from city centres.

Communities of adversity

There will also, of course, continue to be groupings which form in the face of perceived threat to them. Such communities of adversity, while less durable than others, add to the ever-widening range of loose-knit collective opportunities available to individuals. Neighbourhood Watch schemes, for example, have grown in number from one in 1982 to more than 42,000 in 1988. Neighbourhood Watch is 'a community-based activity, supported by local police, that is directed towards crime prevention'. More than 2.5 million households now live within a Neighbourhood Watch area (Edwards 1990, 65).

There are also many activities of citizenship which protect a specific interest. Some agencies and organisations are closely related to and an expression of the community interest they attempt to represent. Some of them represent a very wide interpretation of 'community' and 'the common good'. One example is the Rural Development Commission and other agencies which exist to preserve rural areas as part of national policy. Despite the changes we have described, commitment to village life and the loyalties which they represent remains.

Community Partnerships

Public services increasingly work in partnership with community groups on particular projects. After a careful investigation, Wilmott, in *Community Initiatives – Patterns and Prospects* concludes that community groupings and activities are seen as important partly because there is widening recognition that mediating arrangements are increasingly necessary. This applies most clearly to local territorial communities as illustrated by community architecture, community policing and community care. But 'mediating structures do not have to be local' (Wilmott 1989, 30). The same arguments apply to communities of interest that are not locally based.

This general shift – the 'movement away from centralism and towards a belief in ordinary people' – is sometimes expressed in other terms, such as 'participation', 'empowerment' or 'citizenship' (Wilmott 1989, 30).

Two fundamental aims are increasingly recognised as worthwhile objectives of public policy. 'The first is to help people to come together in meeting their needs and tackling common problems. The second is for public services to strengthen voluntary and informal structures and to work with, rather than against, them' (Wilmott 1989, 31).

Public Services are increasingly using volunteers

The increasing use of volunteers in both the statutory and voluntary sectors is another feature of the change we are describing. The public services which are responsible for hospitals, schools and various kinds of social services increasingly involve volunteers in supportive roles, whether as auxiliary helpers on the hospital wards, providing meals on wheels, or fund raising for the local school. The Women's Royal Voluntary Service, for example, relies on a task force of 160,000 volunteers to deliver an annual 15 million meals on wheels to the elderly and housebound. Many voluntary bodies raise funds for services provided by a combination of professionals and volunteers. The services may meet needs not covered by statutory services, or extend services to groups otherwise uncatered for.

Involuntary participation

The 1984 General Household Survey (GHS) identified around six million carers/helpers in Great Britain, of whom 3.7 million carried the main care responsibility and around 1.4 million devoted 20 hours a week to caring.

Only about half of carers of working age are working even part-time. The Report of the House of Commons Social Services Committee (1990) suggests that between 300,000 and 500,000 carers are below pensionable age, without any income from employment. The Report comments: 'the Government has described the contribution made by carers in the following way: "their total input was greater than the combined inputs financed from central and local government"' (House of Commons Social Services Committee 1990, vii).

The role of independent voluntary bodies is increasing

The role of independent voluntary bodies in providing citizenship entitlements is increasing.

Independent associations or voluntary organisations, many, but not all of which are registered charities, are an important part of our national tradition. Voluntary organisations are defined by the NCVO as 'self-governing bodies of people who have joined together voluntarily to take action for the benefit of the community and have been established otherwise than for financial gain' (NCVO 1990, 16). Those which are not charities are not bound by charity law, and have relative freedom of action. Those which are registered charities are bound by charity law to confine their activities to the objects of their trusts, which may not be changed without permission from the Charity Commissioners.

The role of contemporary voluntary organisations is therefore varied and includes grant-giving, service provision (including advice), self-help or mutual aid, advocacy and campaigning. They range in size from large national organisations at one end of the spectrum, working in partnership with statutory agencies and employing professionals and professional management techniques, to small self-help community groups at the other.

From the foundation of the first anti-slavery society in 1783, to the present day, associations of citizens and trades unions have grown up in response to contemporary social, economic and environmental conditions and concerns. The direct contribution of the Christian Churches to the social needs of the community has been a distinctive element of their ministries for a very long time. In our multi-faith society, other religions and religious institutions such as synagogues and mosques are also active.

The trades unions, which contributed substantially to the attainment of political and social entitlements, continue to be a major promulgator of information about rights, and provide advocates and representatives in individual cases. In 1989, for example, about £150 million was secured in recompense to individuals for industrial injuries.

After the war, the Welfare State assumed many of the philanthropic and charitable functions of the voluntary organisations which had grown up in response to the social conditions caused by industrialisation. This meant that citizens received rights and entitlements to money and services, and there was a corresponding statutory obligation of the State to provide them. Today, that post-war shift from charity to rights is currently being re-examined as efforts are made to control public expenditure. The borderline between the State's responsibilities and those of private citizens and families is being contested in the political arena. Even where there is a clear statutory responsibility embedded in law, there is a move for the state to contract out the provision of services.

Reviewing the range and scope of the voluntary sector, the recent NCVO Report concluded 'these trends have already created for the voluntary sector a change of both scale and kind from a desirable and kindly contribution at the margin of the welfare state to a necessary third force complementing official action on revised social policies and private sector social provision' (NCVO 1990, 54).

> There are new opportunities and new roles for the voluntary sector to play. These will affect the way it works and carries out its activities, its diversity, and its relationship with public and private sectors. Voluntary organisations are also being encouraged to seek out new resources for their work, with Government making it clear that its own responsibility for funding both public services and the sector itself has limits. (NCVO 1990, 19)

3. The Implications of this Changing Pattern

Advantages to institutions of involving volunteers

Evidence seems to suggest that volunteer activity is beneficial to the bodies with which the volunteers are involved:

> Institutions (notably service agencies) that receive volunteers report improved quality of service, better 'tension management' through relieving the staff's work-load, the stimulation of 'staff development' due to the questioning nature of the volunteers, better communication with clients and among staff, and a process of mutual learning. (Weinstein et al 1979; quoted in Halpern, 11)

A second major gain that could potentially emerge from involving volunteers is a reduction in alienation and prejudice.

A volunteer's own work with a group can do much to reduce the volunteer's prejudice towards that group or members of it. Work by the young for the older citizen and by older citizens for the young can reduce alienation. For example, Community Service Volunteers have demonstrated how active involvement can enable young drug addicts or offenders to overcome their own problems.

A third potential gain is greater effectiveness and/or efficiency in the delivery of care. It is important to note, however, that this is not necessarily a cheap option 'as the overt and concealed costs of adequate informal care may yet prove quite substantial' (Bulmer 1985; quoted in Halpern, 19–20).

Fourthly, a long-term gain arises because today's recipients of care frequently become tomorrow's carers. A significant proportion of helpers have themselves experienced similar help from others: 'It would seem that caring for other people can form a positive, self-propagating pattern.' This is evidenced by CSV's work with offenders, many of whom later become volunteers themselves.

Fifthly, there can be a gain to an institution which encourages volunteering both in fostering a positive image in its community and in forging useful outside links.

Advantages to individuals

Research studies suggest that young people benefit personally from a period of volunteering. For example, 'students who volunteered to work with deprived children reported wide-ranging gains, most frequently in self-image – discovering new aspects of self and/or feeling improvement in self-image; in interpersonal relations – positive changes in the ability to work in a team, to give and receive feedback, to relate to authority etc.; and in improved flexibility of thought – the ability to consider things from multiple points of view and see alternatives' (Osterweil and Feingold (1981), quoted in Halpern).

For older people, a more participatory society offers important opportunities. Our society expects the increase in the numbers of pensioners to continue. Many people over 70 today can expect to be as generally healthy as their equivalents of 50 and 60 were in the early post-war years. Yet 'just 5 per cent of [people over 65] are in full time work and 10 per cent in part time work' (50+ Group 1990, 1). At the same time, early retirement is accelerating sharply. Only 57 per cent of men aged between 55-64 years are now in full time employment compared to 87 per cent in 1970.

A key concern for this age group remains poverty. People in retirement are three times more likely to be poor than people in work. Participatory arrangements cannot compensate for social disadvantage. This question is discussed separately in Section II, pages 21–2.

Another concern is the effective exclusion from society of the older generation. People find that 'by arbitrary rulings of age, be it 65, 70 or 75, they are denied opportunities open to others: opportunities to become magistrates or citizen advice workers, drivers or care workers, or opportunities to meet with others and have fun' (50+ Group 1990, 3). The average older person now watches television for 40 hours per week, which amounts to one third of his or her waking life, suggesting perhaps a lack of opportunities.

The 50+ Group, having consulted widely, concluded:

> We believe that voluntary activity, including community involvement, provides older people with an enhanced sense of self-esteem. Older people may take the opportunity to engage in voluntary activity because they recognise that such work will provide an extra dimension to their lives. Voluntary activity provides opportunities to make new social contacts to replace those lost from the paid workplace. Voluntary activity also provides opportunities for mutual aid. Voluntary activity can be not only a source of fun and entertainment but also gives the older person a sense of being useful, of achievement and of structuring their time. It offers sources of information, training and support and presents new challenges as well as maintaining forms of personal development. (50+ Group 1990, 5–6)

No compensation for inadequate services

On the other hand, there is a concern that voluntary effort is being used to compensate for deficiencies in the public services. There are, of course, good examples of organisations comprised both of fully paid staff and unpaid volunteers. But it is important that unreasonable and unrealistic expenditure of time and money should not be expected of voluntary or part voluntary organisations. As an example, we looked at the network of Citizen's Advice Bureaux which has nearly two thousand paid staff and around thirteen thousand volunteers to advise people on their rights and responsibilities and to offer guidance on the services available. Enquiries directly concerning the administration of justice formed a major part of the CABx' work in the last year. They include legal aid and judicial procedures, problems with the police and complaints against solicitors. An example quoted in a recent CAB Report gives a feeling for the kind of work involved:

> On her return from visiting her sick mother in Jamaica a lady had her luggage searched by a customs official. On finding nothing, the customs official took her into a back room where she was strip searched and examined internally. At no time was she informed of

her rights or the reason for the action. She went to her local CAB anxious to find out what could be done about her treatment and, in particular, to get an explanation of it. The CAB secured an apology from the chief customs officer and drafted a letter for her to send to her local MP, who brought the case to the attention of the House of Commons. (NACAB 1989, 13)

Questions of administrative justice complement this work-load. Social security enquiries, for example, formed a quarter of all 7,015,814 questions brought to CAB during 1988/89, to which must be added queries regarding immigration and nationality.

There are many comparable voluntary organisations involved with advocacy, representing clients before tribunals, taking test cases to court to secure legal definitions, establishing rights or campaigning for change. These groups 'undertake research and seek to inform public opinion, influence policy-making and change existing legislation. They supply advice and guidance to those trying to untangle their rights from the web of impersonal bureaucratic procedures in a more friendly and sympathetic way' (NCVO 1990, 17).

We do not believe that voluntary help should be used to compensate for deficiencies in the organisation of a citizenship institution. The confusion of the law and the complexity of social administration not only means that specialist advice is financially costly: it is costly too in volunteer hours, and volunteers are a precious resource. Voluntary help is not an adequate substitute for a simple benefit system or organised public services. The case was well put by Richard Wood, Director of the British Council of Organisations of Disabled People: 'Many, many disabled people do not need caring for, but they are people who are entitled to benefits and they are people who need basic services in order to lead full and independent lives' (House of Commons Social Services Committee 1990, vi).

The Limitations of the Volunteer Contribution

There is a danger in an over-reliance on voluntary effort. There is not an unlimited pool of volunteers:

The first thing that needs to be said is that there is *not* an army of would-be volunteers out there who merely have to perceive a need in order to rush forward and help. Projects designed to encourage volunteering will have to take careful note of what motivates people to become volunteers in the first place. These motivations typically include the desire to be associated with a valued *public* service, and the wish to have clearly-defined role. However, far too many of the roles proposed for volunteers in the community care services seem to stem from a desire to 'fill the gaps' rather than the need to match volunteer motivations with service needs. (MORI 1990, 4)

Established charities are concerned about their ability to maintain voluntary services. More than two-thirds of current volunteers are women in social groups A and B, almost half are between 35 and 54 and most are concentrated in London and the South. Population changes and the large number of women returning to work present serious problems to bodies like WRVS, and to the contribution that individual carers can make. The Department of Employment predicts that 'in the next ten years the female labour force will increase in all regions of the UK and by as much as 21 per cent in some areas. In the South West for example, it is estimated that 79.3 per cent of women of working age will be economically active by the year 2000' (House of Commons Social Services Committee, 1990). Higher activity rates may affect the supply of carers. Alternatively caring may restrict women's availability for paid employment. Whilst economic activity does not necessarily preclude informal care for the less severely disabled, the projections of women's participation in the labour market suggest that there may be a declining number of women willing or able to take on the care role without loss of earnings. The health and social care services are also large employers of women: demographic pressures also affect their ability to recruit suitably qualified staff.

Funding and support for voluntary activities

Voluntary bodies need systematic funding, the use of volunteers costs money and management skills and staff are necessary. Community partnerships may bring dividends to professionals but they require, as we have pointed out, a very careful investment of skill and time: they are not cost free, nor are they yet widespread. Only a minority of local authorities engage in local community development. The need to involve professional community development workers if 'community initiatives are to be promoted in a systematic and coherent way' (Twelvetrees 1989, 42), is often overlooked. We point to Gulbenkian's study of the Parent Organiser Project at Westminster City School as a small but successful example of community partnership. The appointment of a full-time paid parent organiser led to the creation of an effective parent-teacher partnership, involving extensive volunteer contributions to the school. A full-time salaried worker, with support services, as recommended in the analysis by Alan Twelvetrees we referred to, was necessary to establish and maintain this project.

The interests of the volunteers themselves must be safeguarded: volunteers need to be trained, to have a proper role in the organisation they support, to have a relationship with a line manager and to be able to have expenses reimbursed, to be involved in decision-making, and to be treated with as much respect as those doing paid work.

The need for systematic provision

Informal provision or organisation has the advantages of flexibility, efficiency, offering autonomy to workers without distancing them from the organisation's goals, better communication, and job satisfaction. Informal organisations are often local, adding further to the attachment, connectedness, and motivation of their members. In terms of care, this can typically be described as caring motivated by a personal bond. These characteristics, however, have limitations, as well as strengths. Informal or independent associations reflect the interests of their members, which do not necessarily bear any relation to an objectively based pattern of need or entitlement. The strength of a formal system of provision or organisation is that it directs resources to areas or causes most in need, and on the basis of some public (and hopefully accountable) criteria.

Unfortunately, formal systems tend therefore to be impersonal and bureaucratic, but they strive to deliver their service fairly, and on the basis of need or entitlement, rather than personal favour or preference. Clearly the two systems are very different. Each one is a complement to, not a substitute, for the other.

Our investigations demonstrate that the citizenship entitlements of the future in the administration of justice, health and social services will require a formidable combination of individual service, *and* public service, *and* private provision, *and* voluntary service. We have previously argued that a floor of adequate social entitlements should be maintained, monitored and improved when possible by central Government, with the aim of enabling every citizen to live the life of a civilised human being according to the standards prevailing in society. We believe, with the NCVO, that it is important to be clear about the frontier between the proper responsibility of central government so far as the public services are concerned and the proper contribution of independent associations and voluntary bodies. In no sense should voluntary bodies partly or wholly reliant on fundraising and volunteer help take over elements of the core work of the public services. Where voluntary bodies wholly or partly funded by central government offer a basic but supplementary service, then questions arise about how far such a service can be discretionary within local authority areas.

In particular, we argue that there should be a comprehensive citizens' advice service which would include a national advocacy scheme for those disadvantaged groups who cannot claim their own entitlements. Opportunities for volunteers should be more publicised and supported. We refer later to the Commission's 'Volunteers' initiative, which we developed with the Prince's Trust.

Such great questions cannot be settled piecemeal. Two major reviews are called for. The codification of the law and the simplification of social legislation to which we have referred should be accompanied by a major public review co-ordinated by government, of public services and the voluntary sector. Such a review could tackle and report publicly on key policy dilemmas inherent in our evolving arrangements.

We believe that Parliament should consider how it can ensure that the recommendations which are the responsibility of the Central Government can be effectively implemented and independently monitored.

4. Ways of Encouraging Citizenship

Our purpose is to consider how citizens may participate more fully and effectively in society. In our view the removal of impediments, and a greater clarity of roles and purposes within the participatory framework of citizenship entitlements are the essential steps towards this objective. Finally, we turn to the positive measures that might be taken to encourage citizenship.

Schools

Our views on the nature of citizenship studies in school have been submitted to the National Curriculum Council, and are reproduced in Appendix H. So far in the Report, we have considered citizenship studies in relation to knowledge and understanding of how our democratic society works and how it evolved. We believe that the development of skills and experience of community are equally vital components of such an educational experience. Citizenship as a study area is particularly vulnerable either to being presented as theory without practice, as in civic courses, or to being offered solely as an experience, as practice without theory. In the Commission's view, both elements are necessary if a balanced and effective course is to be provided.

Young people should leave a school with some confidence in their ability to participate in their society, to resolve conflict and, if they oppose a course of action, to express that opposition fairly, effectively and peacefully. These skills within school may involve, for example:

- the capacity to debate, argue and present a coherent point of view

- participating in elections

- taking responsibility by representing others, for example on a School Council

- working collaboratively

- playing as a member of a team

- protesting, for example by writing to a newspaper or councillor or local store.

The development of social, planning, organisational, negotiating and debating skills is a major part of this theme.

We also argue that experience within the community is important for the individual, as an encouragement to make a voluntary contribution in later life. Social responsibility, and an awareness of our obligations to consider the impact of our actions and lifestyle on others, helps create an environment in which we can reinforce social cohesion. We were asked to assess methods of recognition. Our consultative conference overwhelmingly supported the contribution of the Record of Achievement in recording and assessing a young person's citizenship contribution. The GCSE in citizenship was equally overwhelmingly rejected, though some Commission members considered that it should not be ruled out altogether for those who wished to pursue it. We believe that the Record of Achievement should have a standard section which enables a simple record to be kept of a young person's achievements in this field, identifying the different elements within the citizenship theme, of understanding, knowledge, skills and community experience.

After School Arrangements

Young people's education is not completed when they leave school. Whether they enter employment, enrol for training or go on to further study, we believe they should have the opportunity to develop their potential as citizens alongside their vital role as workers or potential workers.

The Commission does not see these two strands of development as contradicting one another: indeed they are complementary. With this perspective in mind, the Commission worked with the Prince's Trust to develop 'Volunteers', a scheme which will ultimately, it is hoped, offer every young person the opportunity to join with others for a three-month period in a project emphasising self-development and service to the community. Company representatives, the TUC and a range of voluntary bodies helped in the development of the proposals. Opportunities for longer periods of volunteering or volunteering away from home are offered by Community Service Volunteers. In working with the Prince's Trust to launch this initiative, we maintained the same analysis of the complexity of skills that needed to be learned as we have set out in our approach to citizenship studies in school.

The Community Development Foundation has rightly argued that citizenship is not volunteering alone but 'self-determination and participation in society's decision making processes' (Channon & Lightfoot 1990, 2). We agree with this analysis. All the elements of citizenship should be part of the experience of those who involve themselves with Volunteers, and similar schemes. Nor do we suggest that this is the only way in which individuals can involve themselves. We recognise the contribution of the Youth Service which is developing a core curriculum including citizenship. Again, many young people involve themselves in the community in other ways altogether.

If adequate support is to be made available to enable men and women to organise themselves, and influence decision-making locally and nationally, adult education and community development are of paramount importance. This is true whether groups are organising self-help projects, such as provision and support for young mothers, or whether tenants and residential organisations are seeking to provide facilities and help within their own neighbourhood.

We believe that belonging to a community, which is a core element of citizenship, needs to be fostered; and that ideally all young people should feel they belong and have a contribution of value to make, if they so wish.

Recruitment to Higher Education and work

The post-school experience of many young people is exclusively geared to education, training and work. Individuals' roles as young citizens, if ignored by all the adult institutions, may come to seem irrelevant to the individuals themselves. With this in mind, the Commission decided to find out whether any further encouragements existed for the students to involve themselves in the community or in any other way to demonstrate skills and knowledge of citizenship. Two surveys were conducted in parallel to the survey of schools. The first concerned the attitudes of those who selected students for places in higher education; the second was concerned with the attitudes of those who selected young people for jobs. A summary of the findings is published as Appendix F.

Institutions of higher education seemed to adopt a neutral stance towards participation in the community. It was not a major factor in selection for higher education. That does not imply that the institutions are hostile towards the concept. Many of the pressures that currently operate in the selection process are weighted in favour of traditional academic qualifications, with community participation seen as an additional dimension only. The view of industry and commerce is similar. In recruitment below graduate level, evidence of citizenship is relatively unimportant, but it is slightly more important at graduate level, as it may indicate valuable personal qualities, such as leadership skills. This is not the case everywhere. It is noteworthy that within the United States 'loan forgiveness' exists in certain circumstances for students who have completed a period of voluntary service.

In considering these findings we bore in mind that many young people themselves were taking time off before going into further or higher education, and some were involving themselves in community initiatives during that time. Institutions of higher education, we felt, could perhaps best contribute to creating opportunities for young people to engage in active citizenship by accepting the principle of a break between school and college, and building it into their entry procedures. Many are still reluctant to do so. If, in addition, these institutions formulated explicit selection policies they would have the opportunity to encourage young people by further taking into account their citizenship activities. The UCCA and PCAS forms should, in our view, be amended so that, like the Record of Achievement, they contained a standard section in which a reference to community involvement could be included.

Public attitudes

Companies do frequently allow their staff time off with pay to pursue active citizenship involvement. The activities most commonly allowed for included the Territorial Army, school governorship, blood donation, jury service and lay magistracy. Only occasional references were made in the Commission's survey to making allowances for the prospective parliamentary candidate, local government councillor, charitable work and secondment to the community. Some companies are better placed than others to release staff into the community. Others have facilities they are able to share. Many make financial contributions or work in partnership in a whole range of ways on a voluntary basis.

In a participatory society, the attitude of a company's management to the community is fundamental. We support the lead given by member companies of the Industry and Parliament Trust in developing relations between industry and the community.

We have argued for a society in which individuals participate in part through the exercise of formal entitlements given effect by public institutions and in part through a range of voluntary opportunities. To make a success of that participatory vision, all public institutions need to be prepared to work in partnership. If we value – as the Members of Parliament on the Commission do – the contribution to public life of the lobbying, campaigning, and arguing of individuals and groups that accompanies the decision making and legislative process, then both Government and local government need to be as open as possible in their working and more consistent in their consultative procedures.

Equally, if young people are to be taught the principles of citizenship; then those set in authority over their fellow human beings need to understand them too. The Commission notes the British delegation to the Council of Europe's observations on the place of human rights in the training of some of these key groups:

> Training in the Civil Service is directed at ensuring that civil servants themselves and members of the public with whom they come into contact have their rights under specific statutes observed. The protection of human rights is a key feature of the structure of civil and criminal law.
> ... Although there is at present no formal training component in Human Rights, as such, in either Probationer or Higher Police courses, a high degree of concern for the rights and liberties of the citizen runs as a strong thread throughout all police training in England and Wales.
> Members of the military services receive training in the law of armed conflict including humanitarian law. (Committee of Ministers 1989, 47–8)

We argue that the judiciary, civil servants, teachers, doctors and nurses, local government officers, the police and the armed forces should have specific training on the entitlements and duties of citizens and the corresponding obligations of public institutions as set out in documents such as the European Convention and Social Charter.

Public recognition

We further considered carefully the question of recognition of voluntary contributions. We concluded that, so long as there is an honours system, it should be as supportive of voluntary contributions as it currently is of the work of the diplomatic services, the civil service and the professional classes and professional politicians. We came to the conclusion that a new part of the honours system should be developed to give a distinctive, but equal weight to citizenship and voluntary achievements. We consider that the administration of this new part of the honours system should not be a function of executive government, but ought to be a function of Parliament, and its own institutions. How such a cultural shift could be made lies outside the range of the Commission's work.

The need for a public body

We believe that there is a need for a body charged with the specific responsibility to document and research social, economic and educational aspects of citizenship; to consider new legislation, in relation to the rights and duties of citizenship; and to stimulate informed public discussion. We are therefore in favour of the establishment of either a Standing Royal Commission on Citizenship, or an Organisation with a Royal Charter publishing an annual report, or an Independent Body with a Board of Trustees, to deal with all aspects of citizenship.

5. Conclusion

Neglect of citizenship, of the entitlements and duties of individuals and obligations of institutions, and the quality of participation can damage much that we value in our society. The Commission responded to a widely felt need for this matter to be discussed more openly. We offer two major observations. Firstly, that society is in general best organised through participation and mutual education, both in terms of efficiency and in terms of eventual outcome. The participation of citizens in their society is both a measure and a source of that society's success: democracy and involvement are not, and should not be, reducible to the narrowly political, but concern the very 'business of life'. Secondly, that citizenship is not only about formal rights, but also about the everyday participation in our society; and not only about our own rights, but also about the rights of others. It is this conception of citizenship as both theory and practice that we wish to encourage. We offer this Report as a starting point for a more broad and participatory discussion designed to safeguard citizenship in our changing world.

Encouraging Citizenship

The Report of the Commission on Citizenship

Bibliography

Adult Literacy and Basic Skills Unit (1990) *Youth and Literacy Research* ALBSU

*Barrie, N. Commission on Citizenship: *Paper presented to the Commission on Citizenship Seminar* (April 1989)

Bellah, R.N., Madsen, R., Sullivan, W., Swidler, A., Tipton, S.M. (1985) *Habits of the Heart* University of California Press

Boateng, P. *Unpublished Paper presented to the Commission on Citizenship Seminar* (April 1989)

Bulmer, M. (1986) *Neighbours: the Work of Philip Abrams* Cambridge University Press

Committee of Ministers of the Council of Europe (1985) *Recommendation R(85)7 on Teaching and Learning about Human Rights in Schools* Council of Europe

Committee of Ministers of the Council of Europe (1989) *Committee of Experts for the Promotion of Education and Information in the Field of Human Rights (DH-ED(89)8 Addendum)* Council of Europe

Channon, G. & Lightfoot, J. (1990) *Citizenship, Volunteering and Self-determination* Research and Policy Paper No. 9, Community Development Foundation

*Dahrendorf, R. Commission on Citizenship: *Paper presented to the Commission on Citizenship Seminar* (April 1989)

*Edwards, J. (1990) *Active Citizenship: A Review of the Research Evidence* Commission on Citizenship

50+ Group (1990) *50+ Volunteering* The Volunteer Centre, UK

Fogelman, K. (1990) *Citizenship in Secondary Schools: A National Survey* University of Leicester (published as Appendix E of this Report)

Gardner, P. (1990) *What Lawyers Mean by Citizenship* (published as Appendix D of this Report)

General Household Survey (1981) quoted in Edwards, J. *Active Citizenship: A Review of the Research Evidence*

*Halpern, D. (1990) *Active Citizenship and a Healthy Society* (Commission on Citizenship: Paper prepared for the Commission on Citizenship)

Hansard Society Commission Report (1990) *Women at the Top* The Hansard Society

Henderson, R. *Unpublished Paper presented to the Commission on Citizenship Seminar* (April 1989)

HMSO (1986) 'The Conduct of Local Authority Business: Committee of Enquiry into the Conduct of Local Authority Business' Research Vol II *The Local Government Councillor* HMSO

Hill, M. (1990) *Social Security Policy in Britain* Elgar Publishers

House of Commons Social Services Committee (1990) 5th Report *Community Care: Carers* HMSO

Johnston Conover, P., Crewe, I. & Searing, D. (1990) *The Nature of Citizenship in the United States and Great Britain: Empirical Comments on Theoretical Themes* (article to be published in *Journal of Politics*, Volume 52(4), November 1990)

Jones, C. & Adler, M. (1990) *Can Anyone Get on These? A Report for the Scottish Consumer Council* Scottish Consumer Council

Lister, R. (1990) *The Exclusive Society: Citizenship and the Poor* Child Poverty Action Group

Mayall, B. (1990) *Parents in Secondary Education: The Parent Organiser Project at Westminster City School* Calouste Gulbenkian Foundation, London

Marshall, T.H. (1950) *Citizenship and Social Class* Cambridge University Press

MORI (1990) 'Voluntary Activity: A Survey of Public Attitudes' *Voluntary Action Research Paper No. 1* Volunteer Centre UK

National Association of Citizens Advice Bureaux (1989) *Annual Report 1988/89* NACAB

National Council for Voluntary Organisations (1990) *Effectiveness and the Voluntary Sector – Report of the Working Party* NCVO

National Curriculum Council (1990) *Curriculum Guidance 3: The Whole Curriculum* National Curriculum Council

Osterweil, I.O. & Feingold, H. (1981) *A School Programme for Elementary School Children* School Psycho. Int. 2(3): 30–33

Pateman, C. (1979) *The Problem of Political Obligation: A Critical Analysis of Liberal Theory* John Wiley and Sons

Patten, C. (1990) 7th Arnold Goodman Lecture 'Big Battalions and Little Platoons' delivered on 7th June, 1990 Charities Aid Foundation

*Plant, R. Commission on Citizenship: *Paper presented to the Commission on Citizenship Seminar* (April 1989)

Political and Economic Planning (1947) *Clubs, Societies and Democracy: Planning* Broadsheet No. 263 PEP

Richardson, A. (1990) *Talking About Commitment* The Prince's Trust

Roche, M. (1987) 'Citizenship, Social Theory and Social Change' in *Theory and Society* 16: 363–99 Martinus Nijhoff Publishers, Dordrecht

Smith, A. (1776) *The Wealth of Nations*

Twelvetrees, A. (1989) 'Promoting Community Initiatives – Which Way Forward?' in *Policy Studies* Winter 1989 Vol 10: No.2 PSI

United Nations Development Programme (1990) *Human Development Report 1990* Oxford University Press

Weinstein, R.S., Gibbs, J.T. & Middlestadt, S.E. (1979) 'College Students in Human Service Agencies: Perceptions of their Impact on the Setting' in *American Journal of Community Psychology* 7(2): 209–21 quoted in Halpern, D.

Wilmott, M. (ed.) (1989) *Planning for Social Change – Britain in the 1990's* The Henley Centre

Wilmott, P. (1989) *Community Initiatives: Patterns and Prospects* PSI

The Commission also referred to:
Gaskin, P. and Harris, K. (ed.) (1989) *Active Citizenship: A Bibliography*
Community Projects Foundation, London and the Volunteer Centre UK,
Berkhampstead

* Available from the Secretary to the Commission, 237 Pentonville Road,
London N1 9NJ.

Appendices to the Report

A   Extract from the United Nations Universal Declaration of Human Rights 1948

B   Extract from the Convention for the Protection of Human Rights and Fundamental Freedoms, signed at Rome on 4 November 1950

C   Extract from the European Social Charter 1961

D   J.P. Gardner *What Lawyers mean by Citizenship*

E   K. Fogelman *Citizenship in Schools: A National Survey*

F   J. Francis *Encouraging 'The Typical Volunteer': the Views of Higher Education and Employers*

G   Council of Europe: *Recommendation No. R(85)7 of the Committee of Ministers to Member States on Teaching and Learning about Human Rights in Schools*

H   Commission on Citizenship: *Evidence of the Speaker's Commission on Citizenship to the National Curriculum Council on Citizenship in Schools*

APPENDIX A

Extract from the United Nations Universal Declaration of Human Rights 1948

THE GENERAL ASSEMBLY proclaims

THIS UNIVERSAL DECLARATION OF HUMAN RIGHTS as a common standard of achievement for all peoples and all nations, to the end that every individual and every organ of society, keeping this Declaration constantly in mind, shall strive by teaching and education to promote respect for these rights and freedoms and by progressive measures, national and international, to secure their universal and effective recognition and observance, both among the peoples of Member States themselves and among the peoples of territories under their jurisdiction.

Article 1

All human beings are born free and equal in dignity and rights. They are endowed with reason and conscience and should act towards one another in a spirit of brotherhood.

Article 2

Everyone is entitled to all the rights and freedoms set forth in this Declaration, without distinction of any kind, such as race, colour, sex, language, religion, political or other opinion, national or social origin, property, birth or other status. Furthermore, no distinction shall be made on the basis of the political, jurisdictional or international status of the country or territory to which a person belongs, whether it be independent, trust, non-self-governing or under any other limitation of sovereignty.

Article 3

Everyone has the right of life, liberty and security of person.

Article 4

No one shall be held in slavery or servitude; slavery and the slave trade shall be prohibited in all their forms.

Article 5

No one shall be subjected to torture or to cruel, inhuman or degrading treatment or punishment.

Article 6

Everyone has the right to recognition everywhere as a person before the law.

Article 7

All are equal before the law and are entitled without any discrimination to equal protection of the law. All are entitled to equal protection against any discrimination in violation of this Declaration and against any incitement to such discrimination.

Article 8

Everyone has the right to an effective remedy by the competent national tribunals for acts violating the fundamental rights granted him by the constitution or by law.

Article 9

No one shall be subjected to arbitrary arrest, detention or exile.

Article 10

Everyone is entitled in full equality to a fair and public hearing by an independent and impartial tribunal, in the determination of his rights and obligations and of any criminal charge against him.

Article 11

1. Everyone charged with a penal offence has the right to be presumed innocent until proved guilty according to law in a public trial at which he has had all the guarantees necessary for his defence.
2. No one shall be held guilty of any penal offence on account of any act or omission which did not constitute a penal offence, under national or international law, at the time when it was committed. Nor shall a heavier penalty be imposed than the one that was applicable at the time the penal offence was committed.

Article 12

No one shall be subjected to arbitrary interference with his privacy, family, home or correspondence, nor to attacks upon his honour and reputation. Everyone has the right to the protection of the law against such interference or attacks.

Article 13

1. Everyone has the right to freedom of movement and residence within the borders of each state.

2. Everyone has the right to leave any country, including his own, and to return to his country.

Article 14

1. Everyone has the right to seek and to enjoy in other countries asylum from persecution.

2. This right may not be invoked in the case of prosecutions genuinely arising from non-political crimes or from acts contrary to the purposes and principles of the United Nations.

Article 15

1. Everyone has the right to a nationality.

2. No one shall be arbitrarily deprived of his nationality nor denied the right to change his nationality.

Article 16

1. Men and women of full age, without limitation due to race, nationality or religion, have the right to marry and to found a family. They are entitled to equal rights as to marriage, during marriage and at its dissolution.

2. Marriage shall be entered into only with the free and full consent of the intending spouses.

3. The family is the natural and fundamental group unit of society and is entitled to protection by society and the State.

Article 17

1. Everyone has the right to own property alone as well as in association with others.

2. No one shall be arbitrarily deprived of his property.

Article 18

Everyone has the right to freedom of thought, conscience and religion; this right includes freedom to change his religion or belief, and freedom, either alone or in community with others and in public or private, to manifest his religion or belief in teaching, practice, worship and observance.

Article 19

Everyone has the right to freedom of opinion and expression; this right includes freedom to hold opinions without interference and to seek, receive and impart information and ideas through any media and regardless of frontiers.

Article 20

1. Everyone has the right to freedom of peaceful assembly and association.

2. No one may be compelled to belong to an association.

Article 21

1. Everyone has the right to take part in the government of his country, directly or through freely chosen representatives.

2. Everyone has the right of equal access to public service in his country.

3. The will of the people shall be the basis of the authority of government; this will shall be expressed in periodic and genuine elections which shall be by universal and equal suffrage and shall be held by secret vote or by equivalent free voting procedures.

Article 22

Everyone, as a member of society, has the right to social security and is entitled to realization through national effort and international co-operation and in accordance with the organization and resources of each State, of the economic, social and cultural rights indispensable for his dignity and the free development of his personality.

Article 23

1. Everyone has the right to work, to free choice of employment, to just and favourable conditions of work to protection against unemployment.

2. Everyone, without any discrimination, has the right to equal pay for equal work.

3. Everyone who works has the right to just and favourable remuneration ensuring for himself and his family an existence worthy of human dignity and supplemented, if necessary, by other means of social protection.

4. Everyone has the right to form and to join trade unions for the protection of his interests.

Article 24

Everyone has the right to rest and leisure including reasonable limitation of working hours and periodic holidays with pay.

Article 25

Everyone has the right to a standard of living adequate for the health and well-being of himself and of his family, including food, clothing, housing and medical care and necessary social services, and the right to security in the event of unemployment, sickness, disability, widowhood, old age or other lack of livelihood in circumstances beyond his control.

2. Motherhood and childhood are entitled to special care and assistance. All children, whether born in or out of wedlock, shall enjoy the same social protection.

Article 26

1. Everyone has the right to education. Education shall be free, at least in the elementary and fundamental stages. Elementary education shall be compulsory. Technical and professional education shall be made generally available and higher education shall be equally accessible to all on the basis of merit.

2. Education shall be directed to the full development of the human personality and to the strengthening of respect for human rights and fundamental freedoms. It shall promote understanding, tolerance and friendship among all nations, racial or religious groups, and shall further the activities of the United Nations for the maintenance of peace.

3. Parents have a prior right to choose the kind of education that shall be given to their children.

Article 27

1. Everyone has the right freely to participate in the cultural life of the community, to enjoy the arts and to share in scientific advancement and its benefits.

2. Everyone has the right to the protection of the moral and material interests resulting from any scientific, literary or artistic production of which he is the author.

Article 28

Everyone is entitled to a social and international order in which the rights and freedoms set forth in the Declaration can be fully realized.

Article 29

1. Everyone has duties to the community in which alone the free and full development of his personality is possible.

2. In the exercise of his rights and freedoms, everyone shall be subject only to such limitations as are determined by law solely for the purpose of securing due recognition and respect for the rights and freedoms of others and of meeting the just requirements of morality, public order and the general welfare in a democratic society.

3. These rights and freedoms may in no case be exercised contrary to the purposes and principles of the United Nations.

Article 30

Nothing in this Declaration may be interpreted as implying for any State, group or person any right to engage in any activity or to perform any act aimed at the destruction of any of the rights and freedoms set forth herein.

Extract from the Convention for the Protection of Human Rights and Fundamental Freedoms, signed at Rome on 4 November 1950

The Governments signatory hereto, being Members of the Council of Europe,

Considering the Universal Declaration of Human Rights proclaimed by the General Assembly of the United Nations on 10th December 1948;

Considering that this Declaration aims at securing the universal and effective recognition and observance of the Rights therein declared;

Considering that the aim of the Council of Europe is the achievement of greater unity between its Members and that one of the methods by which that aim is to be pursued is the maintenance and further realisation of Human Rights and Fundamental Freedoms;

Reaffirming their profound belief in those Fundamental Freedoms which are the foundation of justice and peace in the world and are best maintained on the one hand by an effective political democracy and on the other by a common understanding and observance of the Human Rights upon which they depend;

Being resolved, as the Governments of European countries which are like-minded and have a Common heritage of political traditions, ideals, freedom and the rule of law, to take the first steps for the collective enforcement of certain of the Rights stated in the Universal Declaration;

Have agreed as follows:

Article 1

The High Contracting Parties shall secure to everyone within their jurisdiction the rights and freedoms defined in Section I of this Convention.

SECTION I

Article 2

(1) Everyone's right to life shall be protected by law. No one shall be deprived of his life intentionally save in the execution of a

sentence of a court following his conviction of a crime for which this penalty is provided by law.

(2) Deprivation of life shall not be regarded as inflicted in contravention of this Article when it results from the use of force which is no more than absolutely necessary:

(*a*) in defence of any person from unlawful violence;

(*b*) in order to effect a lawful arrest or to prevent the escape of a person lawfully detained;

(*c*) in action lawfully taken for the purpose of quelling a riot or insurrection.

Article 3

No one shall be subjected to torture or to inhuman or degrading treatment or punishment.

Article 4

(1) No one shall be held in slavery or servitude.

(2) No one shall be required to perform forced or compulsory labour.

(3) For the purpose of this Article the term 'forced or compulsory labour' shall not include:

(*a*) any work required to be done in the ordinary course of detention imposed according to the provisions of Article 5 of this Convention or during conditional release from such detention;

(*b*) any service of a military character or, in case of conscientious objectors in countries where they are recognised, service exacted instead of compulsory military service;

(*c*) any service exacted in case of an emergency or calamity threatening the life or well-being of the community;

(*d*) any work or service which forms part of normal civic obligations.

Article 5

(1) Everyone has the right to liberty and security of person. No one shall be deprived of his liberty save in the following cases and in accordance with a procedure prescribed by law:

(*a*) the lawful detention of a person after conviction by a competent court;

(*b*) the lawful arrest or detention of a person for non-compliance with the lawful order of a court or in order to secure the fulfilment of any obligation prescribed by law;

(*c*) the lawful arrest or detention of a person effected for the purpose of bringing him before the competent legal authority on reasonable suspicion of having committed an offence or when it is reasonably considered necessary to prevent his committing an offence or fleeing after having done so;

(*d*) the detention of a minor by lawful order for the purpose of educational supervision or his lawful detention for the purpose of bringing him before the competent legal authority;

(*e*) the lawful detention of persons for the prevention of the spreading of infectious diseases, of persons of unsound mind, alcoholics or drug addicts or vagrants;

(*f*) the lawful arrest or detention of a person to prevent his effecting an unauthorised entry into the country or of a person against whom action is being taken with a view to deportation or extradition.

(2) Everyone who is arrested shall be informed promptly, in a language which he understands, of the reasons for his arrest and of any charge against him.

(3) Everyone arrested or detained in accordance with the provisions of paragraph 1 (*c*) of this Article shall be brought promptly before a judge or other officer authorised by law to exercise judicial power and shall be entitled to trial within a reasonable time or to release pending trial. Release may be conditioned by guarantees to appear to trial.

(4) Everyone who is deprived of his liberty by arrest or detention shall be entitled to take proceedings by which the lawfulness of his detention shall be decided speedily by a court and his release ordered if the detention is not lawful.

(5) Everyone who has been the victim of arrest or detention in contravention of the provisions of this Article shall have an enforceable right to compensation.

Article 6

(1) In the determination of his civil rights and obligations or of any criminal charge against him, everyone is entitled to a fair and public hearing within a reasonable time by an independent and impartial tribunal established by law. Judgment shall be pronounced publicly but the press and public may be excluded from all or part of the trial in the interests of morals, public order or national security in a democratic society, where the interests of juveniles or the protection of the private life of the parties so require, or to the extent strictly necessary in the opinion of the court in special circumstances where publicity would prejudice the interests of justice.

(2) Everyone charged with a criminal offence shall be presumed innocent until proved guilty according to law.

(3) Everyone charged with a criminal offence has the following minimum rights:

(*a*) to be informed promptly, in a language which he understands and in detail, of the nature and cause of the accusation against him;

(*b*) to have adequate time and facilities for the preparation of his defence;

(*c*) to defend himself in person or through legal assistance of his own choosing or, if he has not sufficient means to pay for legal assistance, to be given it free when the interests of justice so require;

(*d*) to examine or have examined witnesses against him and to obtain the attendance and examination of witnesses on his behalf under the same conditions as witnesses against him;

(*e*) to have the free assistance of an interpreter if he cannot understand or speak the language used in court.

Article 7

(1) No one shall be held guilty of any criminal offence on account of any act or omission which did not constitute a criminal offence under national or international law at the time when it was committed. Nor shall a heavier penalty be imposed than the one that was applicable at the time the criminal offence was committed.

(2) This Article shall not prejudice the trial and punishment of any person for any act or omission which, at the time when it was committed, was criminal according to the general principles of law recognised by civilised nations.

Article 8

(1) Everyone has the right to respect for his private and family life, his home and his correspondence.

(2) There shall be no interference by a public authority with the exercise of this right except such as is in accordance with the law and is necessary in a democratic society in the interests of national security, public safety or the economic well-being of the country, for the prevention of disorder or crime, for the protection of health or morals, or for the protection of the rights and freedoms of others.

Article 9

(1) Everyone has the right to freedom of thought, conscience and religion; his right includes freedom to change his religion or belief and freedom, either alone or in community with others and in public or private, to manifest his religion or belief, in worship, teaching, practice and observance.

(2) Freedom to manifest one's religion or beliefs shall be subject only to such limitations as are prescribed by law and are necessary in a democratic society in the interests of public safety, for

the protection of public order, health or morals, or for the protection of the rights and freedoms of others.

Article 10

(1) Everyone has the right to freedom of expression. This right shall include freedom to hold opinions and to receive and impart information and ideas without interference by public authority and regardless of frontiers. This Article shall not prevent States from requiring the licensing of broadcasting, television or cinema enterprises.

(2) The exercise of these freedoms, since it carries with it duties and responsibilities, may be subject to such formalities, conditions, restrictions or penalties as are prescribed by law and are necessary in a democratic society, in the interests of national security, territorial integrity or public safety, for the prevention of disorder or crime, for the protection of health or morals, for the protection of the reputation or rights of others, for preventing the disclosure of information received in confidence, or for maintaining the authority and impartiality of the judiciary.

Article 11

(1) Everyone has the right to freedom of peaceful assembly and to freedom of association with others, including the right to form and to join trade unions for the protection of his interests.

(2) No restrictions shall be placed on the exercise of these rights other than such as are prescribed by law and are necessary in a democratic society in the interests of national security or public safety, for the prevention of disorder or crime, for the protection of health or morals or for the protection of the rights and freedoms of others. This Article shall not prevent the imposition of lawful restrictions on the exercise of these rights by members of the armed forces, of the police or of the administration of the State.

Article 12

Men and women of marriageable age have the right to marry and to found a family, according to the national laws governing the exercise of this right.

Article 13

Everyone whose rights and freedoms as set forth in this Convention are violated shall have an effective remedy before a national authority notwithstanding that the violation has been committed by persons acting in an official capacity.

Article 14

The enjoyment of rights and freedoms set forth in this Convention shall be secured without discrimination on any ground such as sex, race, colour, language, religion, political or other opinion, national or social origin, association with a national minority, property, birth or other status.

Article 15

(1) In time of war or other public emergency threatening the life of the nation any High Contracting Party may take measures derogating from its obligations under this Convention to the extent strictly required by the exigencies of the situation, provided that such measures are not inconsistent with its other obligations under international law.

(2) No derogation from Article 2, except in respect of deaths resulting from lawful acts of war, or from Articles 3, 4 (paragraph 1) and 7 shall be made under this provision ...

Article 19

To ensure the observance of the engagements undertaken by the High Contracting Parties in the present Convention, there shall be set up:

(1) A European Commission of Human Rights hereinafter referred to as 'the Commission';

(2) A European Court of Human Rights, hereinafter referred to as 'the Court'.

APPENDIX C

Extract from the European Social Charter (1961)

The Governments signatory hereto, being Members of the Council of Europe,

Considering that the aim of the Council of Europe is the achievement of greater unity between its Members for the purpose of safeguarding and realising the ideals and principles which are their common heritage and of facilitating their economic and social progress, in particular by the maintenance and further realisation of human rights and fundamental freedoms;

Considering that in the European Convention for the Protection of Human Rights and Fundamental Freedoms signed at Rome on 4th November, 1950, and the Protocol thereto signed at Paris on 20th March, 1952, the Member States of the Council of Europe agreed to secure to their populations the civil and political rights and freedoms therein specified;

Considering that the enjoyment of social rights should be secured without discrimination on grounds of race, colour, sex, religion, political opinion, national extraction or social origin;

Being resolved to make every effort in common to improve the standard of living and to promote the social well-being of both their urban and rural populations by means of appropriate institutions and action,

Have agreed as follows:

PART I

The Contracting Parties accept as the aim of their policy, to be pursued by all appropriate means, both national and international in character, the attainment of conditions in which the following rights and principles may be effectively realised:

1. Everyone shall have the opportunity to earn his living in an occupation freely entered upon.

2. All workers have the right to just conditions of work.

3. All workers have the right to safe and healthy working conditions.

4. All workers have the right to a fair remuneration sufficient for a decent standard of living for themselves and their families.

5. All workers and employers have the right to freedom of association in national or international organisations for the protection of their economic and social interests.

6. All workers and employers have the right to bargain collectively.

7. Children and young persons have the right to a special protection against the physical and moral hazards to which they are exposed.

8. Employed women, in case of maternity, and other employed women as appropriate, have the right to a special protection in their work.

9. Everyone has the right to appropriate facilities for vocational guidance with a view to helping him choose an occupation suited to his personal aptitude and interests.

10. Everyone has the right to appropriate facilities for vocational training.

11. Everyone has the right to benefit from any measures enabling him to enjoy the highest possible standard of health attainable.

12. All workers and their dependents have the right to social security.

13. Anyone without adequate resources has the right to social and medical assistance.

14. Everyone has the right to benefit from social welfare services.

15. Disabled persons have the right to vocational training, rehabilitation and resettlement, whatever the origin and nature of their disability.

16. The family as a fundamental unit of society has the right to appropriate social, legal and economic protection to ensure its full development.

17. Mothers and children, irrespective of marital status and family relations, have the right to appropriate social and economic protection.

18. The nationals of any one of the Contracting Parties have the right to engage in any gainful occupation in the territory of any one of the others on a footing of equality with the nationals of the latter, subject to restrictions based on cogent economic or social reasons.

19. Migrant workers who are nationals of a Contracting Party and their families have the right to protection and assistance in the territory of any other Contracting Party.

What Lawyers mean by Citizenship

J.P. Gardner
Director, The British Institute of International and Comparative Law*

Introduction

1.   The Commission seeks to advocate a development of the present form of citizenship. Before describing in greater detail what that development involves, and what the description of 'active citizenship' implies, it would seem important to set out clearly what citizenship currently means. It is suggested that this should be the starting point for the Commission's further proposals and that a clear description of it should help to expose tensions and weaknesses in the current position and to give pointers to developments which might be desirable.

2.   The short description of the current position which follows is a legal one. Citizenship is an attribute of individuals as members of a political body, but the rules which establish that body and the relationships of individuals to it are legal rules. It is therefore necessary to take account of the rules which make up the legal relationship between individuals and the State which together identify the legal attributes of citizenship. As will be shown, this paper argues that in the United Kingdom the relationship which is described as citizenship is particularly interesting from a legal point of view. A distinction will be drawn between 'nationality citizenship' and 'new citizenship' and it will be suggested that the United Kingdom legal tradition places this country in an enviable position to develop and confirm a new legal interpretation of citizenship which can respond to the international demands arising at the turn

---

* The present paper has been prepared for the Speaker's Commission as a contribution to the Commission's discussion of active citizenship. It derives from research undertaken by the Institute on comparative aspects of citizenship in national law in member States of the European Communities and in certain Commonwealth jurisdictions, as well as on the place of nationality in international law. The principal research has been undertaken by S. Beckwith, A. Boadita-Cormican, D. Chalmers, I. Durgadeen, K. Kenny under the direction of J.P. Gardner.

of the century. It will be argued that the substance of the law has already achieved this aim, but that its complexity and inaccessibility fall short of the standard which would allow citizens to know where they stand.

Citizenship and nationality

3. The traditional legal analysis of citizenship derives in part from the notion of a State in international law. A State in international law is a territory, subject to an authority which is recognised by other States as competent in respect of that territory and the people living there.[1] An attribute of a State, an aspect of its sovereignty, is therefore the ability to confer nationality on its population,[2] a nationality which derives its legitimacy from its acceptance by other States.[3] It follows that States represent and protect the interests of their nationals vis-à-vis other States and that, traditionally, a State is sovereign and uncontrollable in international law in the way in which it treats its own nationals. These are matters which are often thought to fall within the 'reserved domain' of domestic jurisdiction.[4] However it is also thought that the extent of the reserved domain may vary as international law develops.[5]

4. Nationality is the external manifestation of the relationship between individuals and the State to which they belong. When they travel abroad they do so with the authority of a passport issued by the State of which they are a national and in the event of difficulty it is the State of which they are a national which may seek to defend their interests.

5. Citizenship is usually regarded as the reflection of this relationship which applies within the boundaries of the State concerned. It describes the relationship of nationals to their own State when they are within that State. Its functional attributes are to describe matters such as who may vote and stand for election in States which allow democratic activity and often to regulate a large variety of other acts which nationals may do which non-nationals either may never do, or may not do as of right. These activities include owning property, holding certain offices, taking certain jobs and enjoying many economic benefits. This legal relationship, where the enjoyment of various civic rights as a citizen depends upon nationality, is described in the rest of this paper as 'nationality citizenship'.

6. The legal rules which regulate nationality citizenship include those which govern the acquisition, transfer and loss of nationality and the exercise of particular rights, mainly electoral rights, such as

voting and standing for election.[6] The rules may also govern compulsory community service, with the military or otherwise, and are permissive of a significant number of types of employment, frequently including the armed forces, the civil service, teaching and sometimes the whole of public employment. They may also be permissive of residence in a particular territory.

7.   In the case of the United Kingdom the British Nationality Act 1981 defines a British citizen and certain other statutes, such as the Representation of the People Act 1983, refer back to this definition in conferring the right to vote or stand for election, or other enabling provisions. The first codification of the law on nationality and citizenship was the British Nationality and Status of Aliens Act 1914. There is no enumeration of the incidents of citizenship in the 1914 Act or in any subsequent legislation on the subject. Instead, immunity from the various disabilities which attach to alien status[7] provides a 'definition' of the content of British citizenship. The relationship based on nationality is much clearer in certain other countries, as for example in Canada, where the Constitution defines citizens and certain specific rights enjoyed and exercised by them.

Citizenship rights and universal rights

8.   Although this is the traditional analysis of nationality citizenship deriving from the traditional view of the sovereignty of States in international law in relation to their conduct towards their nationals, this view must be modified to take account of developments in international law since the Second World War. Whereas traditionally States and not individuals were legal persons in international law, the atrocities of the thirties and forties led to the recognition of certain limitations and controls on the way in which a State could act towards its own nationals. The Universal Declaration of Human Rights[8] prepared by the United Nations in 1948 was the first major document to recognise these limits. Although the impact of this document, and its progeny,[9] is usually seen in the importance of giving individuals a status in international law, it is also very significant in undermining the assumption that the regulation of the relationship between the State and individuals is mainly concerned with the relationship between the State and its citizens.

9.   The rights which the Universal Declaration identifies, and which have been concretized by the UN Covenants on Civil and Political Rights[10] and on Economic Social and Cultural Rights,[11] as

well as by the European Convention on Human Rights[12] and the Social Charter,[13] are rights enjoyed by everyone. They are human rights because they must be granted to all, without distinction on nationality or any other ground.[14] As a result they are importantly different from the rights which have been described as nationality citizenship rights. Nevertheless they affect a number of very important relationships between the individual (as opposed to the citizen) and the State. In the first place they protect civil and political rights including the prohibition of certain ill-treatment, the control of detention and the protection of privacy, free speech, religion, assembly and fair trial, to name but a few examples. In addition they protect social and economic rights and claims, including property rights, education, employment and benefits. Their significance lies particularly in the fact that they address the content of the legal relationship between the individual and the State, rather than the form. In other words these rights particularly address the position of the disadvantaged, women, the disabled and those subject to discrimination.[15]

10.   The declaration of these rights has been accompanied by their legal interpretation either by domestic courts or by special tribunals established for the purpose,[16] which has quickly identified their practical application and, in certain cases, considerably extended their scope. As a result, these basic rights are very often regarded as central to the relationship between the individual and the State and they have, in many cases, been adopted and included in the written Constitutions of newly independent States. These rights emphasise, not who is defined as belonging to the political entity which is the State in such a way as to be given the right to participate, but what each individual may expect of the State, whatever the individual's degree of involvement with it.

Citizenship in the United Kingdom

11.   In the light of the importance of these rights, which may be described as constituting new citizenship, it is appropriate to consider how citizenship rights are dealt with in the law of the United Kingdom and, in particular, how far the new citizenship rights have been assimilated. As will be seen, the answer to this question lies in part in the way in which nationality citizenship has traditionally been treated in the United Kingdom.

12.   The constitutional settlement of the United Kingdom is based upon the supremacy of the Queen in Parliament. Traditionally,

there are no legal limits to what Parliament can enact as the law of the land. At the same time, as a constitutional monarchy, citizens of the United Kingdom owe allegiance to the Crown in the form of the Sovereign.[17] The origins of this relationship are historical and derive from medieval obligations. Nevertheless they remain significant in the legal relationship which is described as citizenship. The 1914 British Nationality and Status of Aliens Act and subsequent legislation adhered to the traditional methods of acquisition of citizenship through birth, by descent and by naturalisation. However, the first two of these methods, known as the *jus soli* and *jus sanguinis* respectively have been modified by the 1981 British Nationality Act.[18]

13.   The characteristics of that relationship are that the law regulates who 'belongs' sufficiently closely to the political group which is the State to be allowed to take part in the democratic process and to pass that right on to future generations. However, developments over the last fifty years have shed a new light on this legal relationship and have resulted in certain tensions which explain the need to review the scope of citizenship as currently understood. These changes may first be illustrated by the development of Commonwealth citizenship since the Second World War.

The interaction of British citizenship with Commonwealth citizenship

14.   Under the British Empire all subjects of the Crown possessed a single nationality.[19] This was known as the 'common code' of British nationality. With the advent of decolonisation and independence, the Commonwealth became the vehicle for maintaining a legal link between the citizens of newly independent countries and the United Kingdom. However, self-governing dominions began to apply restrictions to the entry of British subjects and some enacted legislation to create separate Dominion citizenships.[20] The Canadian Citizenship Act of 1946 introduced comprehensive Regulation of Canadian Citizenship. This adoption by Canada of its own nationality precipitated a reassessment of the 'common code'. The old system had clearly become unworkable as a means of conferring rights of entry and equality throughout the Commonwealth. A meeting between heads of government took place in 1947, and was known as the Commonwealth Conference. A new twintrack approach was developed. While the independent countries naturally made the rules as to who was and was not a citizen of their country, they also recognised as a special category

citizens of other Commonwealth countries. Many, including the United Kingdom in s.37(1) British Nationality Act 1981, adopted the formal category of Commonwealth Citizen, while other countries specified that reciprocal rights should be enjoyed by citizens of all other Commonwealth countries.

15. This approach explains why in the United Kingdom it is not only British citizens who may vote in Parliamentary and local government elections; the Representation of the People Act 1983 expressly gives the right to vote to Commonwealth Citizens of the Irish Republic.[21] Similar provisions exist in the electoral laws of certain other Commonwealth countries.[22]

16. Initially the United Kingdom was unique in the Commonwealth in also granting the right of entry and residence to all Commonwealth citizens. The Commonwealth Citizens Act 1962 introduced the first restrictions on these immigration rights, which have since become far more stringent.[23] As a result, the citizenship relationship has been undermined in practice although the legal attributes of citizenship are still recognised for Commonwealth citizens who are able to become resident in this country.

17. As this example illustrates, in the United Kingdom citizenship has not been regulated by reference to 'nationality citizenship'. Key aspects of the formal relationship between individuals and the State, such as voting have not depended on holding British citizenship. On the other hand, the right of residence, which is often regarded as an attribute of nationality citizenship, has increasingly not been enjoyed by a significant group of individuals whose nationality status depends upon, or is regulated by, the British Nationality Act 1981. It may therefore be said that during the last forty years the United Kingdom has moved away from the nationality citizenship model.

Citizenship rights and residence

18. The legal rules governing nationality can be described as the most limited aspect or 'level' of citizenship. Another level is that of rights and duties which may arise by virtue of a person's residence in a particular area, irrespective of that person's nationality.

19. Aliens are entitled to avail of certain rights, which can be broadly classed as 'social and economic rights', while resident in the U.K. These rights include the right to treatment under the National Health Service,[24] supplementary welfare benefit[25] and social security.[26] A local education authority is under a duty to bestow on

persons who are 'ordinarily resident in the area of the authority' awards in respect of attendance on certain educational courses.[27] None of these provisions is restricted to British citizens or Commonwealth citizens *per se* although obviously it must be presumed that in order to take up residence and avail of them most aliens will have complied with any applicable immigration requirements.

The significance of the European Communities for citizenship rights

20.   The traditional legal relationship between the people and Parliament has been significantly amended in another fundamental respect. Membership of the European Communities has brought with it the economic right for British citizens to work in any Community country and for their citizens to seek work and set up businesses here.[28] At the same time, the European Communities Act 1973 recognised the supremacy of European Community law over the law of England and Wales, Scotland and Northern Ireland. Although theoretically this Act could be repealed by Parliament if the United Kingdom were ever to leave the European Communities, while it is in force it provides a restriction of the powers of Parliament and constitutes an exception to the traditional assumption that Parliament is free to legislate at will.

21.   The economic development of the European Communities into a single unit is advancing quickly as the Internal Market is established. Many people in other European Community countries, and many in the United Kingdom too, see this economic development as one step towards the declared aim of the European Communities of ever closer union, and ultimately of a European political unit. While any such development must lie in the future, it is noticeable that the European Communities' main competence is in economic matters.[29] As a result, those who enjoy freedom of movement to seek jobs or to establish businesses are essentially the economically active rather than the whole citizenry. Even among the economically active there are distinctions as to the extent to which benefits intended to facilitate free movement of workers may be availed of by different types of persons. In relation to co-ordination of social security measures, for example, it has been noted that there are three levels of 'citizen': the regular worker, the long-term unemployed and the non-worker.[30] Furthermore, economic migrants from other Community countries do not enjoy

political rights in this country, even though, as a workmate or employer, they are *de facto* citizens. The Immigration Act 1971, on its face, seems to class nationals of European Community countries in the general category of non-patrials. However, the Immigration Rules provide for the entry of such persons to the UK without the requirement of a work permit or prior consent. European Community nationals are, strictly speaking, classed as aliens as a result. As such they are less well protected by national constitutional safeguards and in some instances by supranational guarantees of human rights.[31]

22.   As time passes and the movement of workers between Community countries becomes no more unusual than Scots working in England or than English working in Wales, this democratic deficit may not be sustainable. This is especially clear when it is remembered that the reason for establishing the Communities in the first place was to prevent national control of coal and steel production and thereby to guarantee peace and democracy in Europe. A pointer in this direction is provided by the regulation of candidacy and voting for the elections to the European Parliament. It is clear that the introduction of a uniform system of voting for these elections will both reflect a common approach to the institution itself, and show that allowing non-nationals to vote in elections is not a revolutionary step. The practice has existed in a limited form in the United Kingdom as well as in certain other European countries for many years.

The treatment of 'new citizenship' rights in Europe and the United Kingdom

23.   As well as a common democratic tradition, the European countries also share other common basic values about the relationship of the individual and the State. These common attitudes will facilitate contact between the citizens of European Community countries who will more easily feel at home in one another's jurisdictions. Nevertheless, in one important respect, the traditional constitutional analysis of our omnicompetent and all-powerful Parliament is somewhat anachronistic when compared with the position in most other European Community countries. While the values such as free speech and privacy are shared throughout Europe, the way in which they are protected is different in most countries from the British model.

24.   Under the British Constitution the rights which individuals can exercise without State interference are not usually defined. Instead, the authorities' powers are defined, and various acts which individuals might commit are prohibited, As a result, the individual's rights are residual; individuals are free to do what is left over after laws have imposed piecemeal restrictions where Parliament thought them necessary.[32] So it is sometimes said that individuals can do anything which is not prohibited. However, with the enormous increase in the power and activities of Government since the Second World War, the individual is often concerned not with the areas which Parliament has 'left alone', but with challenging the extent to which the authorities encroach on rights which the individual thought he had.

25.   Claims of this kind are particularly important in the United Kingdom in view of the progressive rejection of nationality citizenship. Where nationals enjoy specific rights by virtue of that status it is sufficient for individuals to be clear about their nationality entitlement in order to be confident of enjoying the rights which go with it. However, as citizenship rights are increasingly defined without reference to nationality, it becomes more important to concentrate on the scope of the specific rights which are granted. The question therefore arises as to how well the law in the United Kingdom responds to new citizenship.

26.   The treatment of the rights which make up new citizenship is very different in most other European countries from that in the United Kingdom. Many of them have a legal tradition of expressly recognising the rights of individuals. Often rights such as freedom of speech or privacy are contained in a written Constitution or another document. The definition and scope of each right still depends on the interpretation given to it by the courts, but the right itself exists to be claimed. Express conferral or recognition of a right in written form clarifies for the individual his position in relation to the State. It is difficult to determine the precise parameters of a right (or duty) where it only exists to the extent that it has not been curtailed by written legislative measures. An expression of the limits to which a right may be curtailed by legislative or other methods may accompany a written guarantee of that right. This provides further clarification. In real terms, written and unwritten rights may be co-extensive in their scope of application. However, the citizen's awareness of the existence of a particular right, its applicability in a given circumstance and hence the likelihood that the right will be availed of are bound to increase where that right is given written expression.

The place of the European Convention on Human Rights

27.   Many new citizenship rights are protected by the European
Convention on Human Rights, a treaty which the United Kingdom
helped to draft and to which it is a party. The Convention allows for
individuals to complain to the European Commission of Human
Rights in Strasbourg [33] and cases may then be decided by the
European Court of Human Rights. Although many countries have
included the Convention in their national law, the United Kingdom,
like the Scandinavian countries, has not. However, all other parties
to the Convention have either incorporated it or have a domestic
written bill of rights. Some have both. Hence, in a number of cases,
the Human Rights institutions in Strasbourg have had to consider
arguments about these rights in the United Kingdom for the first
time, which the UK courts have not been able to consider. In a few
instances the United Kingdom has actually been found to have
violated the rights in the Convention and the law has subsequently
been amended so that the problem cannot recur. The result is to add
to the patchwork of legal provisions affecting the relationship
between the individual and the State which lies at the heart of
citizenship. Furthermore, redress for the infringement of a right
protected by the Convention but not by national law must be sought
through Convention institutions. Municipal courts tend to refuse to
adjudicate on the basis of a norm which has not been incorporated
into the municipal law.[35]

28.   Some argue that the Convention should be made part of the
law in the United Kingdom. Others suggest that its terms are too
broad, or its approach is too vague and that the present piecemeal
approach is the best, notwithstanding the parliamentary delays in
preparing and enacting legislative changes. This debate raises very
fundamental constitutional arguments about the powers of
Parliament, the role of the judges and the importance of
international agreements. Whichever way the debate is ultimately
resolved, it highlights a more general issue namely how a legal
system should respond to new citizenship.

The impact of the internal Market

29.   In view of the growing complexity of governmental persons
and their scope, it is clearly essential that the individual's legal
position vis-à-vis the State should be clear. In the past, the essential
relationship was defined in terms of nationality citizenship. That
model is no longer suitable both because it has been undermined as

a matter of legislative practice in the United Kingdom and because it did not address a sufficient range of rights or deal with the increasingly important question of the relationship between the State and individuals who are lawfully present and involved in the activities of the community, but who are not necessarily nationals – the *de facto* citizens. This group has assumed, and will continue to assume, increasing significance due to the development of the European Communities. Nationals of Community countries already enjoy the right of establishment and hence *de facto* citizenship in the economic sphere: as the Internal Market moves to conclusion the effect of workers' freedom of movement will progressively increase.

30.   The legal relationship between individuals and the State also has a social dimension. The right to education and to adequate health treatment must be considered as well as the right to free speech and other civil rights. Like the civil rights, these social rights are part of a common European heritage. Their common acceptance is an essential prerequisite for the economic co-operation which the Internal Market represents. If social provision was widely different in different parts of the European Community, the 'common market' would be distorted. The European Community institutions are given little direct competence in the field of education, with the exception of vocational training.[36] However, inter-governmental co-operation has taken place in this area[37] and, in principle, persons exercising their rights of free movement should be granted equal access to national educational facilities.[38] This clearly places some 'citizens' in a position which benefits more from European Community provisions than others. Non-national education may only be availed of by persons with a right of residence in a particular member State.[39] This excludes school children and students who have not entered the labour market.

31.   As regards matters of social security, the EEC restricts itself to co-ordination rather than harmonisation of national measures. The result is that there are no centrally determined substantive provisions. There are no common rules, merely common objectives. Two general aspects of social security provisions are dealt with. Firstly, it is sought to establish a personal rather than a territorial basis for the application of social security laws. The aim is for benefits to follow the individual who moves from state to state. Secondly, the European community seeks to ensure the equal treatment of men and women in the award of social security benefits. However, without a centrally devised definition of equality upon which to base a principle of non-discrimination, it has been

73

possible for member states to implement 'equal' treatment in a manner which maintains or even reduces previous levels of expenditure.[40] Thus, in real terms 'new citizenship' can amount to different things in different member states.

The need for 'accessible' law

32. In certain respects the legal arrangements between the State and the individual which can adapt to these changes are already in place in the United Kingdom. The rights to education and National Health Service treatment, as already mentioned, are examples of such arrangements. Nevertheless in the area of social benefits, as well as with areas of traditional civil rights, the position is less straightforward. The enabling legislation, where it exists, is notoriously complex and frequently only intelligible to those administering the scheme or to a specialist adviser.[41] In certain areas of civil rights law, the position rests on case law, some of which is outdated and conflicting. As a result more than one of the findings of breaches of the European Convention on Human Rights has been based on the absence of a clear legal basis for particular aspects of the relationship of the individual and the State.

33. This problem of obscurity of the citizenship relationship is accentuated when it is recalled that new citizenship emphasises the effective enjoyment of rights in practice i.e. the content as well as the form of the legal relationship between individuals and the State. The test of accessibility of the law is not therefore whether a specialist lawyer can advise on the question with accuracy. It is whether the individual who needs to rely upon the protection or benefit which the law provides, can understand it. Democratic participation requires that the law should be simple and accessible: that people should know where they stand.

Conclusion: citizens must know where they stand

34. The legal relationship between individuals and the State is complex in Britain. It reflects an extraordinary period of constitutional continuity during which gradual evolution has been the hallmark of change. The result is a system with many virtues, many of which have been enhanced rather than reduced in the evolutionary process. Notwithstanding the positive attributes of these arrangements, changes in the political and economic

74

circumstances of the country suggest that the form of the existing model may no longer be the best. For example, the decline in importance of Commonwealth citizenship has been achieved not by direct amendment, but by the superimposition of different categories of citizen. Additional requirements must then be satisfied before Commonwealth citizens can effectively enjoy their potential rights in this country. Although the political justification for this has been fully debated from time to time, the consequence has been to create a complex legal situation which is difficult for the ordinary person to master. The same criticism can be made of the way in which the United Kingdom ensures respect for certain fundamental human rights or social entitlements: the legislation is piecemeal and the resulting patchwork of rights is inaccessible and confusing.

35.   The shift in emphasis away from nationality citizenship has arisen at the same time as a general recognition that the State must respect a broader range of rights in its dealings with all individuals. This new citizenship has both a substantive and a formal aspect. Although these rights are mainly protected in the law of the United Kingdom, they are inaccessible both because there has been no systematic treatment of them, and because making the law intelligible to the layman has not been given a high priority. Legislation in the United Kingdom is drafted to serve two purposes: first to inform the members of the Houses of Parliament of the purpose and effect of Bills and secondly to provide a logical, coherent statement of the law for the 'user'.[42] Reconciling these aims is not easy but would be facilitated if a 'textual' method of amending legislation were adopted instead of the present incorporation by reference method. This would make a loose-leaf statute book a possibility, into which amendments to an Act could be inserted.[43]

36.   An extreme imaginary example may illustrate the difference. Let us assume that the Dog's Act 1890 provides:

> 'Section 1 – Any person who keeps a dog shall obtain a licence in accordance with the following provisions . . .

It is now proposed to introduce cat licences on the same basis as the dog licence scheme. The reference system might produce the following result:

> Miscellaneous Provisions Act 1990
> 'Section 1 – In section one of the Dogs Act 1890 the words 'and or cat' shall be inserted after the word dog.'

The textual method might involve the enactment of the Cats and Dogs Act 1990 setting out the text of the relevant provisions in full.

If a loose-leaf statute-book were in use, an amending act might allow the replacement of the page containing section 1 of the 1890 Act with a page containing the amended version of the section. Explanatory material which would not form part of the amending legislation could be provided. The process of naming statutes could also be co-ordinated.

37.   The complexity of the reference approach is illustrated in respect of the British Nationality Act 1981 by section 7(1) of that Act which deals with the right to register as a citizen by virtue of residence in the UK or relevant employment. It states:

'7(1) A person shall be entitled, on an application for his registration made (subject to subsections (6) and (7)) within five years after commencement, to be registered as such a citizen if either of the following requirements is satisfied in his case, namely –
(a) that, if paragraphs 2 and 3 (but not paragraph 4 or 5) of Schedule 1 to the Immigration Act 1971 had remained in force, he would (had he applied for it) have been, on the date of the application under this subsection, entitled under the said paragraph 2 to be registered in the United Kingdom as a citizen of the United Kingdom and Colonies; or
(b) that, if section 5A of the 1948 Act (and section 2 of the Immigration Act 1971 as in force immediately before commencement) had remained in force, he would (had he applied for it) have been, both at commencement and on the date of the application under this subsection, entitled under section 5A(1) of the 1948 Act to be registered as a citizen of the United Kingdom and Colonies.'

It has been suggested that '. . . the British Nationality Act 1981 has created new injustices and anomalies, many of its provisions are so obscurely drafted that they are unfit to be in the statute book.'[44]

38.   It is recognised that the implementation of these suggestions would initially involve substantially increased work for draftsmen who are already hard pressed. Nevertheless, in the longer term, increased clarity would reduce other costs.

39.   In this attitude the United Kingdom is out of step with other European countries where the tradition of codification has been based on the assumption that the law should be accessible to all. The United Kingdom has traditionally been generous in protecting the individual against the State. This may be illustrated on a domestic and an international level, with the ratification of both the European Convention on Human Rights and the Social Charter, with the specific legal obligations which both impose. The response which is needed now to complete the reception of new citizens into

the law of the United Kingdom is not reform of the law, but a major effort to simplify it and improve its accessibility.

Footnotes

1. Brownlie, 'Principles of Public International Law', 73–6; 90–93.
2. Rousseau, 73 Hague Receuil (1948 II), 239–46.
3. Brownlie, *supra*. note 1, 284–6.
4. Tunis and Morocco Nationality Decrees, P.C.I.J. Ser.B., No.4 (1923), 24.
5. *The Nottebohm Case* (1955) I.C.J.Rep. 231: A State's determination that a particular individual is a national is not conclusive. It must comply with principles of international law as to the existence of genuine links with the state concerned.
6. Eg UK, Representation of the People Act 1983, ss. 1 & 2; Australia, Commonwealth Electoral Act 1918–1973, s.39; Canada, Elections Law, ss. 50–53, Canadian Constitution Act, 1982, s.3.
7. Eg Aliens Restriction Act 1914; Aliens Restriction (Amendment) Act 1919; Aliens Employment Act 1955; Immigration Act 1971; British Nationality Act 1981.
8. UN GA Res. 217 (III), 10 December 1948.
9. Eg. European Convention on Human Rights (1950) ETS, No. 5; UNTS Vol. 213, 221.
10. U.K.T.S. 6 (1977), Cmnd 6702; in force 1976.
11. U.K.T.S. 6 (1977), Cmnd 6702; in force 1976.
12. *Supra* note 9.
13. U.K.T.S. 38 (1965), Cmnd 2643; in force 1965.
14. Eg. under Article 2 Universal Declaration of Human Rights, *op.cit.* the rights are stated to be guaranteed to all 'without distinction of any kind, such as race, colour, sex, language, national or social origin, property, birth or other status'; also Andrew Drzemczewski, 'The position of Aliens in Relation to the European Convention on Human Rights', 1985, Council of Europe Directorate of Human Rights.
15. *Ibid.*: see also Article 14, European Convention on Human Rights, *supra* note 9; Articles 2 and 3, International Covenant on Civil and Political Rights, *supra* note 10.
16. Special Tribunals include: European Court and Commission of Human Rights (European Convention on Human Rights); Human Rights Committee (International Convention on Civil and Political Rights). These two treaties also require state parties to provide effective domestic remedies for violations of the rights and freedoms which they protect.
17. Allegiance was owed to the crown derived from birth (*jus soli*), connection through birth (*jus naturalis*) and from naturalisation, *Calcins case* (1608) 7 Rep. 1a.46; *Johnstone v. Pedlak* [1921] 2 AC 262.
18. C.C. Turpin, 'British Nationality and the Right of Abode 1948–83', The Cambridge Tilburg Law Lectures, fifth series, 1982 (Kluwer, 1985).
19. British Nationality and Status of Aliens Act 1914 provided for a unified system of naturalisation of aliens and for common rules for the acquisition of British subject status.

20. Eg Canada, 1921; South Africa, 1927; The Irish Free State, 1935.
21. ss. 1 and 2.
22. *Supra* note 6.
23. See Commonwealth Immigrants Act 1968; Immigration Act 1971.
24. National Health Service Act s.1, the Secretary of State is responsible for the provision generally free of charge of services for the physical and mental health of the 'people' of England and Wales.
25. Supplementary Benefits Act 1976 s.1 (1), benefit available to 'every person' in Great Britain of or over the age of 16 whose resources are insufficient to meet his requirements.
26. Social Security Act 1975 s.2(1), the meaning of 'employed earner' is 'a person who is gainfully employed in Great Britain'.
27. Education Act 1962 s.1 (as substituted by the Education Act 1980 s.19 sch.5).
28. Article 3 EEC Treaty.
29. Although Article 2 EEC Treaty makes specific reference to social objectives.
30. Linda Luckhaus, 'EEC, Social Security and Citizenship', Paper presented at the W.G. Hart Legal Workshop on the Single European Market and the Development of European Law, 1989.
31. Christopher Vincenzi, 'Towards a Citizen's Europe', Paper presented at the W.G. Hart Legal Workshop on the Single European Market and the Development of European Law, 1989; Andrew Drzemczewski *supra* note 14.
32. Walker v. Baird [1892] AC 491, only those restrictions which are authorised by statute may validly be placed on the subject.
33. Subject to a declaration by the state against whom the complaint is lodged that it recognises the competence of the commission to receive individual petitions. Article 25 of the Convention.
34. Article 48. Note that individuals may not petition the court directly.
35. Eg *In Re O'Laighleas* [19 . .] Irish Reports (*The Lawless Case*) where the Irish Supreme Court refused to hear an argument on the provisions of the convention after an argument based on Irish written constitutional provisions was found inadmissible.
36. Articles 128 and 235 EEC Treaty.
37. Eg the establishment of European schools and the European University Institute through intergovernmental agreement.
38. Article 49 EEC Treaty; Regulation 1612/68.
39. Julian Lonbay, 'Educational Rights', Paper presented at the W.G. Hart Legal Workshop on the Single European Market and the Development of European Law, 1989.
40. Linda Luckhaus, *supra* note 30.
41. For a summary of public opinion as to the accessibility of social security see: 'Reform of Social Security', Background Papers presented to Parliament by the Secretary of State for Social Services, June 1985 (HMSO) Cmnd 9519.
42. 'Statute Law: the Key to Clarity' (1972), 15; 'State Law: A radical simplification' (1974), 39, Statute Law Society publications by Sweet & Maxwell.
43. See generally Statute Law Society publications *ibid* and 'Statute Law Deficiencies' (1970):
44. Anthony Lester, 'The Constitution: Decline and Renewal' in *The Changing Constitution* (Jowell and Oliver ed.) 1989 Oxford, Clarendon Press, 345 and 351–2 (with reference to s.7(1)).

Citizenship in Secondary Schools: A National Survey

Professor Ken Fogelman
School of Education, University of Leicester*

A Summary Report

Citizenship in Secondary Schools: A National Survey

In the Autumn term of 1989, 455 secondary schools throughout England and Wales completed questionnaires on their activities relevant to citizenship. Undertaken on behalf of the Speaker's Commission on Citizenship, this is the first survey to provide a representative national picture of how this topic is being tackled in our schools, both within and beyond the formal curriculum. The availability of this evidence is timely, not only for the Commission's deliberations, but also because of the imminent publication of the National Curriculum Council's guidelines on Citizenship as a cross-curricular theme.

This preliminary summary of findings has been prepared primarily for a national consultative conference of schools, taking place in Northampton on February 16th, 1990. A fuller report is in preparation.

Sample and Questionnaire

The questionnaire was distributed to a random sample of 800 maintained secondary schools throughout England and Wales. It was returned, and completed in time to be included in this analysis, by a total of 455, a response rate of 57%. Given the extremely tight timetable and the many other demands on schools this is a very

* This survey was undertaken on behalf of the Speaker's Commission on Citizenship, and funded by Esso UK. Piloting fieldwork and data analysis were carried out by Social and Community Planning Research as part of a programme of research on citizenship under the management of Professor Ken Fogelman of the School of Education, University of Leicester, who also prepared this summary.

The national consultative conference on citizenship in schools, held in Northampton on February 16th, was organised by the Centre for the Study of Comprehensive Schools, University of York (Tel. 0904 433240).

satisfactory response, in itself indicating the high level of interest and enthusiasm for this topic in many schools.

The questionnaire contained four main sections. The first asked for background information about the school, and the answers confirm the general representativeness of the sample. For example, 84 per cent of responding schools were comprehensive and 85 per cent co-educational. Just under half contained pupils from age eleven through to eighteen, and one third eleven to sixteen.

The remaining three sections of the questionnaire covered students' involvement in community activities and service organised by the school; teaching within the school on subjects, topics and issues concerned with community and citizenship; and student participation in the decision-making structures of the school. Where appropriate, detailed information was obtained separately for each year group within the school, but this summary concentrates on two year groups, the twelve to thirteen-year-olds and the fifteen to sixteen-year-olds, in order to give both an overall picture and the contrast between two age groups which differ in terms of whether they are at the stage of preparing for the GCSE at sixteen.

Community Activities and Services

For each year group schools were offered a list of possible activities and asked to indicate those in which their students were involved. Table 1 summarises the results for the two year groups mentioned above.

Table 1 Proportions of schools with pupils involved in specified activities

	12–13 yr olds %	15–16 yr olds %
Activity		
Visiting or helping people		
– the elderly in their homes	15	40
– the elderly in hostels/hospitals	8	40
– people with disabilities	8	22
– ill people in hospitals	3	40
– people in other health care situations	1	11
– children in nursery or primary schools	5	24

	12–13 yr olds %	15–16 yr olds %
Other work for voluntary or statutory services or bodies:		
– environmental projects	22	18
– fundraising for charity (organising, taking part, *not* just giving money)	86	26
– clerical or office help	3	1
– catering	5	1
Other activities	3	2
No pupils in the year group participating in such activities	10	3

The most immediately striking result is the very small proportion of schools where no pupils were involved in some such activities – just one in ten for the twelve to thirteen-year-olds, and fewer than one in thirty for the fifteen to sixteen-year-olds. For the younger children, by far the most popular activity is fundraising (but it should be noted that this involved some activity beyond simply giving money). In fact for 43 per cent of schools this was the only activity reported for this age group.

For the older pupils, greater involvement in a wider range of activities is reported, with particular emphasis on working with the elderly, the disabled and young children.

Of course, these figures alone tell us only that some pupils were involved in these activities, not how many nor how regularly. These two issues were addressed in the next two questions. For twelve to thirteen-year-olds, one third (33 per cent) of the schools with some involvement reported that all or nearly all of their pupils participated in these activities. A further 24 per cent said that more than half did so, and in only 18 per cent was the proportion a quarter or fewer. For fifteen to sixteen-year-olds the comparable figures were 29 per cent all or nearly all; 17 per cent more than half; and 36 per cent a quarter or fewer.

When asked to state the regularity of participation of most of their pupils, one in five of the schools, for both age groups, were unable to give a straightforward answer because it varied too much from pupil to pupil.

A further indication of the greater activity of older pupils is that just 12 per cent of schools with some participation reported that the involvement of most of their fifteen to sixteen year-olds was on just one or two occasions, whereas 29 per cent reported regular participation over a term or more (the remainder falling between these two extremes). For twelve to thirteen-year-olds the figures were almost reversed, with 10 per cent of schools claiming most of their pupils were involved regularly for at least a term, and 29 per cent saying that this was on only one or two occasions.

Not surprisingly, given their different position in relation to formal examination preparation, the way in which these activities were organised differed markedly between the two groups. Although for both age groups, about one in five of the schools indicated that these activities took place out of school hours, for the younger students only 5 per cent said that these activities took place within main curriculum subject lessons whereas 34 per cent did so for the older students. For the fifteen to sixteen-year-olds 26 per cent of schools stated that these activities took place within a work experience placement.

There is a keen debate about whether and how community activities by young people at school should be rewarded. Until recently it seemed likely that recognition and reporting of such activities would be part of a national records of achievement scheme, but it now appears that the statutory element to be reported will be limited to the National Curriculum assessment. As far as current practice is concerned, the replies from schools identify a great variety of ways in which student participation in community activity is recognised, as is shown in Table 2. Schools were asked to identify all methods which they used, so the figures in the table add to more than 100 per cent.

Table 2 Methods of reporting on and assessing community activity

	12–13 yr olds %	15–16 yr olds %
Community activity not reported on or assessed	13	7
Contributes to public exam	0	29
Part of other formal award scheme (Scouts, Duke of Edinburgh etc)	2	26
Contributes to record of achievement scheme:		
– self assessment report	21	49
– teacher assessment report	12	41
Other reports to parents	13	27
References for employers	1	63
Applications or references for Higher or Further Ed.	1	38
Items in school assembly	49	53
Items in press, school magazine	47	59
Other	2	4

For the younger age group, informal methods predominate, with almost half of schools mentioning items in assembly, the press or school magazine. Although no other one method is mentioned very frequently, only 13 per cent of schools state that community activities are not reported on or assessed at all for this age group.

It is clear that more formal assessment of such activities is much more common for the fifteen to sixteen-year-olds. Items in assemblies and the press etc. are still mentioned by more than half of the schools, but for more than a quarter these activities contribute to public exams or some other formal award. Most frequently reported is references to employers (by 68 per cent). That the figure of inclusion in references to Higher or Further Education is somewhat lower (38 per cent) may simply reflect that this is less appropriate for this age group. Among schools with seventeen to eighteen-year-olds involved in community activities, 60 per cent said that these were reported in such references.

Citizenship studies within the school

The next section of the questionnaire was concerned with the place of citizenship within the school's curriculum. Schools were asked to report on 'subjects, topics or issues concerned with community and citizenship that can be broadly defined as political, civil and social rights and duties'.

Some insight into the importance which a school places on this area of the curriculum can be inferred from how it is managed within the policy and management structures of the school. 43 per cent of schools reported that they had an agreed policy or curriculum document or written statement particularly about citizenship studies within the school, although for only 5 per cent was this a separate document rather than part of some wider curriculum document.

Schools also varied in where responsibility for citizenship within the curriculum was placed. 21 per cent stated that it was co-ordinated or overseen by a member of the school's senior management team, and in a further 18 per cent some other member of staff had a specific responsibility for this area. In the remainder implementation depended on the initiatives of particular departments or teachers.

Schools were asked to indicate, again separately for each year group, what specific topics falling within their definition of citizenship/community studies were taught in the past year. The range of replies was far too great to attempt any systematic summary here, but some examples may help to give a flavour of the great variety of topics being covered by schools which are relevant to citizenship.

Twelve to thirteen-year-olds:

nature conservation; charity involvement; pollution; the
Christian community; support for the third world; health and
safety; the family; relationships; making choices; voting and the
parliamentary system; police and policing; the aged; alcohol
education; eating for health; recreation; smoking; skills for
adolescence; people who serve our community; third world
communities; personal safety; decision making; lifestyles;
money management.

Fifteen to sixteen-year-olds:

world of work; health morals; conflict and reconciliation in the
community; national and international affairs; trades unions;
duties and rights of adults; family responsibility; social
awareness; the media; the school and the community; mental
health studies; sexual relationships and decision making;
persecution and prejudice; using local agencies; body abuse;
local government; parliament; child care; crime and crime
prevention; consumer awareness; population growth; care of
elderly people; handicap in the community; respect for the
environment; child development; youth cultures.

Correspondingly, there is variety in the subject areas within
which these topics are covered by schools. When asked to identify
all the relevant subject areas in which they were taught, as many as
11 per cent indicated that they taught Citizenship as a separate
subject within the curriculum. More frequently it was included in
more familiar subject areas such as History, Geography and
Humanities (78 per cent), Home Economics (62 per cent), English
(60 per cent), Business Studies (45 per cent), Economics (28 per
cent) and Social Studies (28 per cent). Also frequently mentioned as
areas in which aspects of citizenship were covered were CPVE
(Certificate of Pre-vocational Education) courses (37 per cent) and
BTEC Foundation Studies (24 per cent). In addition 77 per cent
reported that some aspects were covered in form time or tutorial
groups. However most frequently mentioned of all was PSE
(Personal and Social Education), by 95 per cent of schools.

When asked to identify the *one* subject area within which most
citizenship studies teaching took place for *most* pupils, PSE was by
far the most frequently selected by schools (67 per cent). The only
other subject areas mentioned by significant numbers were form
time (15 per cent) and Humanities (9 per cent). Only 1 per cent (i. e.
4 schools) indicated that citizenship as a separate subject was their
main method.

84

A specific question was put to the schools on the amount of classroom time which was spent on citizenship and community studies. Table 3 summarises their responses for the two selected age groups.

Table 3. Amount of classroom time spent on community/citizenship studies

	12–13 yr olds %	15–16 yr olds %
None	14	2
1–5 lessons a year	24	10
Regular (at least once a week) lessons for half a term	7	8
Regular lessons for one term	4	4
Regular lessons for two terms	1	2
Regular lessons through the year	43	46
Varies according to subject options	6	27

The table suggests substantial variation among schools, but for both age groups the most common situation is of regular lessons throughout the year. The figures for the older students are a little difficult to interpret as, not surprisingly at this age, more than a quarter of the schools stated that classroom time varied according to subject options. Nevertheless, it is noteworthy that only 2 per cent of schools reported no classroom time at all for the subject with this age group, compared with 14 per cent at twelve to thirteen.

Almost all schools (99 per cent) reported that they had, in the past year, brought visiting speakers into the school to work with classes or groups of pupils. Most frequently mentioned were representatives of the Police or Fire Services (90 per cent of schools), followed by the Churches (76 per cent); smoking, drinking or drug abuse advisers (69 per cent); other voluntary organisations or charities (63 per cent); sex/contraceptive use advisers (51 per cent); environmental groups (47 per cent); the Local Authority (42 per cent); other health advisers (34 per cent); political parties (29 per cent); and pressure groups (14 per cent).

Pupil Representation

Many teachers would argue that, in preparing young people to take their place as adult citizens, the general ethos of the school, as exemplified by relationships between staff and students and pupils' involvement in decisions, is at least as important as what is taught or experiences of community activity. A more sensitive exploration of these areas was beyond the scope of this survey, but the opportunity was taken to ask about pupil representation and participation in a number of respects. The answers to these questions are summarised below:

%

(a) schools which organise mock (political) elections — 54

(b) schools which have a school council or year or house councils, on which pupils are represented — 60

(c) those with a school council etc, for which pupil members are elected by the student body — 97

(d) those with a school council etc, on which all year groups are represented on the council(s) — 70

(e) schools with pupil representation at meetings of the School Governors:

regularly — 13
sometimes — 8

(f) schools with pupil representation at meetings of the PTA or equivalent body:

regularly — 9
sometimes — 14

(g) schools with pupil representation on any other body or committee — 25

The other bodies or committees described under (g) were very varied. Several schools referred to a prefects' or sixth form committee. Among other examples given were: charity committee; local crime prevention panel; police advisory committee; local schools consortium; marketing group; farm management group; book committee; Soviet exchange committee; school mini-bus appeal committee; action group to fight school closure.

Schools' use of volunteers

A final set of questions, which do not fit neatly into the preceding sections, but which may also give some insight into schools' attitudes and opportunities in this area, and are also relevant to the more general debate on voluntary activity, concerned the schools' own use of volunteers. Three quarters of the schools reported that, in the academic year 1988–89, volunteers (possibly including parents) had come in during school hours to help with some aspect of the school's work.

Of those, 29 per cent stated that such help was regular, and 22 per cent that it was a mix of regular and occasional help, leaving 49 per cent for whom it was occasional only.

Perhaps surprisingly, in 41 per cent of these schools (i.e. in 31 per cent of all the schools in the survey) this included help in the classroom. 26 per cent (of all schools) reported volunteers helping with individual pupils; in 54 per cent they were helping with the library, outings or sport; and in 20 per cent with administration or preparing materials.

Future work

The above is very much a summary, preliminary report. In particular it concentrates on two age groups within the schools. The fuller report now being prepared will be able to present findings on the full range of age groups. In addition it will examine whether and how activities in the schools vary according to some of their characteristics, such as whether they are situated in an inner city of rural area.

January 1990

Encouraging 'The Typical Volunteer': the views of Higher Education and Employers

J.C. Francis

1. Introduction

The aim of the Commission is to consider how best to encourage, develop and recognise Active Citizenship within a wide range of groups in the community both local and national including school students, adults, those in full employment as well as volunteers.

In order to discover the extent of Active Citizenship in Britain a major review of recent research evidence was undertaken[1]. While the 'popular' view is that many voluntary activities are undertaken by young people (certainly, much publicity is given to organisations which promote voluntary work by young people), the research evidence showed that in fact the typical volunteer was aged between 35 and 44 years and in employment. This paper examines firstly, the views of institutions of higher education who supply, *inter alia*, the labour market. Secondly, we review the attitudes of the employers – who not only recruit graduates and non-graduates, but also influence the career paths of their employees. In this respect we are concerned with the way in which employers support (or otherwise) the development of active citizenship amongst their employees.

Firstly, we look at the way in which higher education regards active citizenship.

2. The View of Higher Education

What responsibility do institutions of higher education have in encouraging the development of active citizenship through their selection procedures? It could be argued that if higher education encourages active citizenship when selecting students, this attitude could filter through into employment and play a part in the career development of middle and senior managers. Thus the encouragement of active citizenship could be seen as a routine activity.

In a survey of a sample of institutions of higher education undertaken by the Commission[2], the results demonstrated a neutral approach to the recognition and valuing of active citizenship. Most departments took no account of voluntary service in selecting candidates. The only exception was in the selection of candidates for degrees including sociology, particularly but not exclusively in courses leading to careers in social work or social administration. Of these, 68 per cent of departments took voluntary work into account in the selection of candidates.

In those departments which took into account in the selection process that students had undertaken voluntary service, many departments stated that it was of minor importance. There was no indication that it was used more in selecting mature rather than younger candidates, or more in initial selection than in second screening. Higher admissions officers commented that the question of the usefulness of voluntary service as a selection factor *had never been raised*.

It was rare for a candidate's attention to be drawn in advance of the admission interview to the fact that departments involved in social administration and social work placed a value on voluntary service in selection. Usually these departments asked about voluntary service during the interview. There was a difference between universities and non-university institutions of higher education in that half of all departments in non-university institutions took voluntary service into account compared with a quarter of the university departments. The difference is largely accounted for by the importance placed on voluntary service as a selection factor by departments teaching sociology in the non-university sector. If these departments are excluded then only a third of the non-university departments took account of voluntary service.

2.1   Some Optimistic Signs

With respect to voluntary service the position of higher education is one of neutrality. If voluntary service is largely not a factor in selection for higher education that does not imply the institutions are hostile towards the concept. Many of the pressures that currently operate in the selection process are weighted in favour of traditional academic qualifications with voluntary service as an additional dimension.

There are however some positive signs. With a subject like sociology there is a clear link between voluntary service and the business of the subject which is to do – in the broadest sense – with people. Beyond that, as the participation rate in higher education is increasing, new criteria – themselves more broadly based – will be necessary for entry to more diverse patterns of degree courses. It is noted that as Records of Achievement become more common, the characteristics of the whole person will become more important, compared with purely academic qualifications.

3. The View of Industry

There is a wealth of evidence demonstrating the amount of work being undertaken by industry and commerce to support community and social life. Large companies have social responsibility funds contributing to charitable work in the community, they fund education-industry liaison and undertake sponsorship of their own staff (again, mostly young people) on initiatives such as Operation Raleigh.

3.1 Employers' Response to 'Volunteers' – a new Initiative for 1990

In a survey of responses to The Prince's Trust Consultation Paper 'Young Volunteers in the Community'[3], over 15 per cent of companies stated that they already had a full commitment to encouraging active citizenship programmes through their existing funding. Some, but not all, of these companies who are seriously committed to their corporate support of active citizenship endorsed the young volunteers in the community proposals and stated that they were prepared to become involved. There is a ceiling for some employers on their ability to support such ventures. Overall three-quarters of the companies endorsed and one-third of the employer organisations stated that they would be prepared to be involved in the scheme by funding and/or releasing their employees for a period of full-time or part-time action as volunteers in the community.

Barriers to involvement were: the difficulty in sparing volunteers away from the job, particularly as young employees were in scarce supply; the shortage of funds to second volunteers and to pay for their replacements; and an unwillingness to act until government support for the scheme was clear.

3.2 Survey of Industry on Active Citizenship

In order to discover what the attitude of employers was to the encouragement of active citizenship, the Commission asked the Industry and Parliament Trust (IPT) to conduct a survey of its member companies[4].

The IPT, whose concern is to promote involvement by business and industrial personnel in local government and national political life, has fifty or so member companies and represents over 2.3 million employees and a total turnover of £150,000 million pounds. A questionnaire to member companies (66 per cent response rate) showed the following results:

3.2.1   In general the most important indicator for selection was a candidate's examination results, involvement in active citizenship being of secondary significance. With respect to recruiting graduates there was a tendency for companies to place equal value on evidence of active citizenship as on examination results.

3.2.2   About 80 per cent of the companies recognised that a period of voluntary service or similar active citizenship involvement was a valuable indicator for recruitment purposes. When companies were asked why they valued active citizenship they indicated that it included the skills of leadership, working with people, self-reliance, 'get up and go', resistance to stress, commitment to the community and travel experience.

3.2.3   When asked what kind of recognition or accreditation could be given to active citizenship, companies were not enthusiastic about using the examination system, i.e. to award grades for citizenship. It was felt that active citizenship involvement should indicate a willingness to help rather than a desire for another qualification to be put on the CV. Evidence of the motives for involvement and the skills obtained thereby were more important than formal recognition.

3.2.4   A number of companies were reluctant to recognise active citizenship as part of their recruitment and selection procedures as it could be interpreted negatively, suggesting somebody would be less committed to their job because of their interests in other (voluntary) activities. When asked what might encourage these major companies to take more account of active citizenship in recruitment, a number of responses indicated that there would need to be a change in company policy and public recognition for companies that encouraged active citizenship. For small companies it was particularly important that employees did not spend too much time away from work.

3.3 Career Development and Active Citizenship

3.3.1 The companies were asked whether they currently allowed their staff time off with pay to pursue active citizenship involvement. The responses here showed that the activities most commonly allowed for included the Territorial Army, school governorship, blood donation, jury service and lay magistracy. However, with many of these the company has no choice but to comply with the request. Only occasional references to making allowances for the prospective parliamentary candidate, local government councillor, charitable work and secondment in the community, were made. One company mentioned that political activity indicated personal ambition which could be counter-productive to employment.

3.3.2 A crucial question related to the level of positive encouragement to take part in citizenship activities given by companies to existing employees and what effect this had on career progression and promotion. Companies were equally divided on this issue. The positive companies did so for the same reason that they took active citizenship into account for recruitment purposes. Even so, several of these said that career progression ultimately depended upon performance in the job. Those that were negative tended to emphasise that performance in work was the only criterion that was recognised.

3.3.3 It is encouraging to note that three-quarters of the companies prepared their employees on pre-retirement programmes to become involved in active citizenship.

4. Facilitating Active Citizenship by Companies

At least two organisations which facilitate active citizenship at a corporate level were identified by the survey conducted by Janet Edwards[1]. Firstly, Action-Match, which exists to promote social sponsorship as a fund-raising/marketing technique and to show companies and voluntary organisations how they can work together for mutual benefit.

Secondly, Action Resource Centre (ARC), which works particularly to promote secondments from industry into the voluntary sector. The goal is to transfer business skills and resources to community organisations in order to enhance their effectiveness in determining the economic and social development of their neighbourhoods. The change and renewal in the inner city must, ARC believes, benefit those who live there and must engage them in the process.

It was recognised by the IPT (when it met with the Commission to discuss the survey) that companies had a problem in balancing the time spent by their personnel in direct community involvement with the demands of the business. It was noted however that a number of companies have established practical and equitable arrangements, e.g. Grand Metropolitan have just published a 21 page brochure entitled 'Grand Metropolitan in Partnership with the Community'. United Biscuits have published 'Community Link', an 8 page colour review of the companies' community activities. IBM's '10 per cent Rule' is a scheme by which staff may take the equivalent of half a day a week for voluntary activities in the community. However, the clear distinction needs to be made between a company which is sponsoring community and social projects through decisions taken at Board level (an activity which is increasingly evident in both large and small companies) and the much more 'risky' practice of allowing individual staff to take time off work to undertake voluntary activities of their choice, which may include 'whistleblowing'. Secondment of personnel onto community work still tends to be seen as part of the lead up to retirement rather than a mid-career activity.

Only to a limited degree do companies see the active involvement of their personnel in the community as providing positive benefits to the individual which are then recognised and/or used by the company. Indeed, for their own part, staff in companies tend to believe that any involvement by them in local or national political life will be regarded negatively by their employer.

As 'enlightened self-interest' had resulted in steadily increasing school-industry links, so the same criterion could apply to personnel involvement in the community in general, particularly as regards local and national political life. A greater emphasis on mid-career community involvement would be of considerable advantage to the company and the individual.

There is a need to change attitudes within companies towards involvement of their staff in the community. Given that much business and industrial share ownership is held by the investment institutions the following statement is of particular significance:

As the largest institutional investor in Grand Metropolitan, Norwich Union represents more than 2 million representatives, each ultimately, with a personal stake in the success of the company. I am certain that they will share my satisfaction that Grand Metropolitan's outstanding record of growth and profitability is complemented by a genuine commitment to put so much back into the communities which have helped the company to thrive.
(E.M. Sandland, Chief Investment Manager, Norwich Union)

5. The Typical Volunteer

In the survey conducted by Janet Edwards[1], the typical volunteer was most likely to be employed (not out of work or retired), to be between 35 and 44 years of age, to be in a high socio-economic professional group, to have spent longer in full time education, to have high educational qualifications, to be involved in raising money, committee, or organisational work and giving practical help to individuals.

These will be the characteristics of the very people who are applying for higher education courses and looking for rewarding career opportunities in business, commerce and industry, and the civil service. Thus there are far-reaching implications for the encouragement and recognition of active citizenship by higher education and companies (particularly major public companies). Clearly, these institutions can play a major role in developing active citizenship or neutralising or discouraging it.

6. Conclusion

Bluntly, if only in terms of the self-interest of the employers or of the institutions of higher education, in order to attract and retain the appropriate calibre of personnel, they will have to meet both the instrumental (job-related) needs and the effective (social and emotional) needs of their personnel. This will certainly require provision for and encouragement of staff to take part in voluntary work, in fulfilling their role as active citizens: an entitlement not a negotiated option.

Recommendations

1. Those companies which have policy guidelines should give greater publicity within their organisation and externally about their policies regarding their existing corporate community involvement and the involvement of individuals in the community.
2. Companies should consider the formulation of such policies if they do not exist.
3. An award should be instituted, by the Speaker, to recognise those companies which made outstanding contribution to the community.

4. Institutions of higher education should be explicit to their policies on using evidence of active citizenship involvement as part of their recruitment process.
5. Approaches should be made to UCCA, SCUE, CNAA and CVCP regarding the value placed on the use of such evidence.

References

1. Active Citizenship. A Review of the Research Evidence. Janet Edwards (1989).
2. Voluntary Service – A Factor in Selection for Higher Education. A Paper commissioned by the Commission on Citizenship. Malcolm Deere and Mary Hallaway (1989).
3. Young Volunteers in the Community: A Consultation Paper. The Prince's Trust and the Commission on Citizenship (February 1990).
4. Report of Survey of IPT Members. Unpublished Paper by Industry and Parliament Trust. Frederick R Hyde-Chambers (1989).

June 1990

Council of Europe: Recommendation No. R(85)7 of the Committee of Ministers to Member States on Teaching and Learning about Human Rights in Schools*

The Committee of Ministers, under the terms of Article 15.*b* of the Statute of the Council of Europe,

Considering that the aim of the Council of Europe is to achieve a greater unity between its members for the purpose of safeguarding and realising the ideals and principles which are their common heritage;

Reaffirming the human rights undertakings embodied in the United Nations' Universal Declaration of Human Rights, the Convention for the Protection of Human Rights and Fundamental Freedoms and the European Social Charter;

Having regard to the commitments to human rights education made by member states at international and European conferences in the last decade;

Recalling:

— its own Resolution (78) 41 on 'The teaching of human rights',
— its Declaration on 'Intolerance: a threat to democracy' of 14 May 1981,
— its Recommendation No. R(83)13 on 'The role of the secondary school in preparing young people for life';

Noting Recommendation 963 (1983) of the Consultative Assembly of the Council of Europe on 'Cultural and educational means of reducing violence';

Conscious of the need to reaffirm democratic values in the face of:

— intolerance, acts of violence and terrorism;
— the re-emergence of the public expression of racist and xenophobic attitudes;
— the disillusionment of many young people in Europe, who are affected by the economic recession and aware of the continuing poverty and inequality in the world;

---

* Adopted by the Committee of Ministers on 14 May 1985 at the 385th meeting of the Ministers' Deputies.

Believing, therefore, that, throughout their school career, all young people should learn about human rights as part of their preparation for life in a pluralistic democracy;

Convinced that schools are communities which can, and should, be an example of respect for the dignity of the individual and for difference, for tolerance, and for equality of opportunity,

I.   Recommends that the governments of member states, having regard to their national education systems and to the legislative basis for them:

(*a*) encourage teaching and learning about human rights in schools in line with the suggestions contained in the appendix hereto;

(*b*) draw the attention of persons and bodies concerned with school education to the text of this recommendation;

II.   Instructs the Secretary General to transmit this recommendation to the governments of those states party to the European Cultural Convention which are not members of the Council of Europe.

Appendix to Recommendation No. R(85)7

Suggestions for teaching and learning about human rights in schools

1.   Human rights in the school curriculum

1.1. The understanding and experience of human rights is an important element of the preparation of all young people for life in a democratic and pluralistic society. It is part of social and political education, and it involves intercultural and international understanding.

1.2. Concepts associated with human rights can, and should, be acquired from an early stage. For example, the non-violent resolution of conflict and respect for other people can already be experienced within the life of a pre-school or primary class.

1.3. Opportunities to introduce young people to more abstract notions of human rights, such as those involving an understanding of philosophical, political and legal concepts, will occur in the secondary school, in particular in such subjects as history, geography, social studies, moral and religious education, language and literature, current affairs and economics.

1.4. Human rights inevitably involve the domain of politics. Teaching about human rights should, therefore, always have international agreements and covenants as a point of reference, and teachers should take care to avoid imposing their personal convictions on their pupils and involving them in ideological struggles.

2.   Skills

The skills associated with understanding and supporting human rights include:

    i. *intellectual skills,* in particular:

— skills associated with written and oral expression, including the ability to listen and discuss, and to defend one's opinions;

— skills involving judgment, such as:

  – the collection and examination of material from various sources, including the mass media, and the ability to analyse it and to arrive at fair and balanced conclusions;

  – the identification of bias, prejudice, stereotypes and discrimination;

    ii *social skills,* in particular:

— recognising and accepting differences;

— establishing positive and non-oppressive personal relationships;

— resolving conflict in a non-violent way;

— taking responsibility;

— participating in decisions;

— understanding the use of the mechanisms for the protection of human rights at local, regional, European and world levels.

3.   Knowledge to be acquired in the study of human rights

3.1. The study of human rights in schools will be approached in different ways according to the age and circumstances of the pupil and the particular situations of schools and education systems. Topics to be covered in learning about human rights could include:

    i.   the main categories of human rights, duties, obligations and responsibilities;

    ii. the various forms of injustice, inequality and discrimination, including sexism and racism;

    iii. people, movements and key events, both successes and failures, in the historical and continuing struggle for human rights;

    iv. the main international declarations and conventions on human rights, such as the Universal Declaration of Human Rights and the Convention for the Protection of Human Rights and Fundamental Freedoms.

3.2. The emphasis in teaching and learning about human rights should be positive. Pupils may be led to feelings of powerlessness and discouragement when confronted with many examples of violation and negations of human rights. Instances of progress and success should be used.

3.3. The study of human rights in schools should lead to an understanding of, and sympathy for, the concepts of justice, equality, freedom, peace, dignity, rights and democracy. Such understanding should be both cognitive and based on experience and feelings. Schools should, thus, provide opportunities for pupils to experience effective involvement in human rights and to express their feelings through drama, art, music, creative writing and audiovisual media.

4. The climate of the school

4.1. Democracy is best learned in a democratic setting where participation is encouraged, where views can be expressed openly and discussed, where there is freedom of expression for pupils and teachers, and where there is fairness and justice. An appropriate climate is, therefore, an essential complement to effective learning about human rights.

4.2. Schools should encourage participation in their activities by parents and other members of the community. It may well be appropriate for schools to work with non-governmental organisations which can provide information, case-studies and first-hand experience of successful campaigns for human rights and dignity.

4.3 Schools and teachers should attempt to be positive towards all their pupils, and recognise that all of their achievements are important — whether they be academic, artistic, musical, sporting or practical.

5. Teacher training

5.1. The initial training of teachers should prepare them for their future contribution to teaching about human rights in their schools. For example, future teachers should:

    i. be encouraged to take an interest in national and world affairs;

    ii. have the chance of studying or working in a foreign country or a different environment;

iii. be taught to identify and combat all forms of discrimination in schools and society and be encouraged to confront and overcome their prejudices.

5.2. Future and practising teachers should be encouraged to familiarise themselves with:

i. the main international declarations and conventions on human rights;

ii. the working and achievements of the international organisations which deal with the protection and promotion of human rights, for example through visits and study tours.

5.3. All teachers need, and should be given the opportunity, to update their knowledge and to learn new methods through in-service training. This could include the study of good practice in teaching about human rights, as well as the development of appropriate methods and materials.

6. International Human Rights Day

Schools and teacher training establishments should be encouraged to observe International Human Rights Day (10 December).

Commission on Citizenship: Evidence of the Speaker's Commission on Citizenship to the National Curriculum Council on Citizenship in Schools

Outline Conclusions of the Commission on Citizenship to be Submitted to the National Curriculum Council

1.   Basis of Recommendation

The submission of the Commission on Citizenship to the National Curriculum Council on the place of Citizenship within the school is set out in detail in the following documents:

(i)   National Survey of Schools conducted by Leicester University and SCPR for the Commission.

(ii)   In depth survey of schools conducted by Leicester and Northants LEAs and Leicester University for the Commission.

(iii)   Report of the Consultative Conference on Citizenship in Schools organised by the Centre for the Study of Comprehensive Schools, for the Commission.

(iv)   Talking About Commitment: SCPR Research into the attitudes of young people undertaken on behalf of the Prince's Trust and the Commission.

(v)   Council of Europe Document R(85)7 on the teaching of Human Rights in school.

(vi)   The first section of the Report of the Commission on Citizenship, reviewed in the light of the Consultative Conference.

2.   Purpose of the Outline Conclusion

The purpose of this note is to highlight briefly some points from the documentation which are of particular relevance to the deliberations of the National Curriculum Council. The note is not a substitute for the set of documents submitted, which, taken together, constitute the evidence which the Commission wishes to submit to the NCC.

3. Citizenship Education for Every Child

(i) Document R(85)7 sets out the view of the Council of Ministers that 'throughout their school career all young people should learn about human rights as part of their preparation for life in a pluralistic democracy'.

(ii) Secretary of State for Education John MacGregor MP and Shadow Spokesperson Jack Straw MP on February 16th at Northampton publicly endorsed the need for citizenship to be taught in schools.

(iii) Young people, for example in the SCPR document, have clearly indicated the importance they attach to this area of their education.

(iv) The Speaker of the House of Commons established the Commission in part because of his concern that young people should know how they are governed and be able to participate in their society.

(v) The Commission strongly supports the case for citizenship studies to be a part of every young person's education whether in state or private sector schools, irrespective of the course of study being followed, and from the earliest year of schooling and continuing into the post school years within further and higher education and the youth service.

(vi) The Commission welcomes the National Curriculum Council's decision to issue guidance to schools in this matter.

4. Citizenship as a Theme and Area of Study

(i) The study of citizenship involves
  - understanding the rules
  - the acquisition of a body of knowledge
  - the development and exercise of skills
  - learning democratic behaviour through experience of the school as a community, and from the experience of the school as an institution playing a role in the wider community.

(ii) Citizenship as a study area is particularly vulnerable either to being presented as theory without practice, as in civic courses, or to being offered solely as an experience, as practice without theory. In the Commission's view all the elements set out in 4(i) are necessary if a balanced and effective course is to be provided.

5. Values and Attitudes

(i)   The Council of Ministers recommends that the main international charters and conventions to which the UK is signatory should provide the reference points, within the classroom, for the study of citizenship.

(ii) The Commission's Report supports this view: however, the Commission feels that the development of entitlements and responsibilities within the UK should also be a feature of the curriculum.

(iii) The differences of approach within these traditions should be brought out and their relative merits discussed.

6. Citizenship as a Body of Knowledge

(i)   The Commission's survey strongly indicates that though the title of citizenship exists within the curriculum plans of many schools there is wide variation in understanding of what the title means, and provision is patchy.

(ii) In the Commission's view it is vital that the NCC guidance clarifies this question for schools.

(iii) The Council of Ministers Document R(85)7 sets out a framework of relevant ideas.

(iv) The first section of the Commission's Report offers a definition of citizenship, and a similar delineation of the civil, political and social entitlements and responsibilities it entails, and the nature of the democratic order it assumes. The relevance of the individual's involvement in the community is developed in this context, and the relevance of the voluntary contribution considered.
This section of the Commission Report was discussed in detail by the 700 participants to the Commission conference. The text has been amended to take account of the views expressed.

(v)   The Commission suggests that these two texts may be helpful in this context.

7. The Place of Citizenship Within the Curriculum

(i)   The framework of the curriculum has already been determined. Within that framework it is likely that citizenship will be taken forward within core and foundation subjects such as English, History or Geography and in parallel as an element in Personal and Social Education.

103

(ii) There is a real danger that:
  (a) citizenship will continue to be ill-defined;
  (b) the theme will lack status by comparison with core and foundation subjects;
  (c) it will become 'lost' within the curriculum;
  (d) its organisation and development will be neglected.

(iii) In the Commission's view NCC guidance must deal realistically with this problem; a viable curricular mapping and audit strategy is vital if the management of a school are to ensure the proper delivery of this topic. As part of the audit strategy the LEA should have a clearly specified responsibility for monitoring and reporting on delivery by schools in their area.

8.   Skills

(i)   A number of the documents submitted deal with the skills of citizenship. The Commission regards the element of acquisition of skills as crucial to the success of the citizenship theme; young people should leave a democratic school with some confidence in their ability to participate in their society, to resolve conflict and, if they oppose a course of action to express that opposition fairly, effectively, and peacefully. These skills within school may involve, for example:
- the capacity to debate, argue and present a coherent point of view
- to participate, for example, in elections
- taking responsibility by representing others, for example on the School Council
- working collaboratively
- playing as a member of a team
- protesting, for example by writing to a newspaper or councillor or a local store.

The development of social, planning, organisational, negotiating and debating skills is a major part of this theme.

9.   Experience of Community

The school is a community. Equally it exists within a series of wider communities. The Commission, in its Report, has argued that in a society with a healthy democratic tradition, the importance of the voluntary contribution of citizens to their own society is recognised and encouraged by the citizens themselves and by the public and private institutions within it. This section of the Commission Report was strongly endorsed by the consultative conference.

The voluntary, in this sense, embraces a wide variety of activities from the magistracy or membership of the local council, to membership of a local pressure group campaigning against a council proposal or involvement in organisations that raise uncomfortable issues for authority. For many people it involves activities which support and complement – but do not replace – local caring services, for example working alongside professionals in hospitals, or with those suffering from disabilities, or with the elderly in the community.

The Commission is strongly of the view that the experience of citizenship involves empowering the individual within her or his community and the school through its arrangements and relationships should foster that development.

10. Recognition and Assessment

The consultative conference overwhelmingly supported the contribution of the Record of Achievement in recording and assessing a young person's citizenship contribution. The GCSE in citizenship was equally overwhelmingly rejected though the Commission members continued to feel it should not be ruled out altogether for those who wish to pursue it.

The Commission believes that the Record of Achievement should have a standard section which enables a simple record to be kept of a young person's achievements in this field, identifying the different elements within the citizenship theme.

Conclusion

Citizenship should be an integral part of every young person's education: the Commission hopes that every school will respond to the guidance of the National Curriculum Council, and give this theme the weight it deserves within the planned experience of schooling offered to the student.

22 March 1990

Printed in the United Kingdom for HMSO.
Dd.293605, 9/90, C30, 3385/4, 5673, 120266.